South Lancashire
Edited by Steve Twelvetree

To Ganny and Pops

Merry Christmas!

With all my love

Olivia xxx

(pg 95)

2004

Young Writers

First published in Great Britain in 2004 by:
Young Writers
Remus House
Coltsfoot Drive
Peterborough
PE2 9JX
Telephone: 01733 890066
Website: www.youngwriters.co.uk

All Rights Reserved

© Copyright Contributors 2004

SB ISBN 1 84460 517 5

Foreword

Young Writers was established in 1991 and has been passionately devoted to the promotion of reading and writing in children and young adults ever since. The quest continues today. Young Writers remains as committed to engendering the fostering of burgeoning poetic and literary talent as ever.

This year's Young Writers competition has proven as vibrant and dynamic as ever and we are delighted to present a showcase of the best poetry from across the UK. Each poem has been carefully selected from a wealth of *Once Upon A Rhyme* entries before ultimately being published in this, our twelfth primary school poetry series.

Once again, we have been supremely impressed by the overall high quality of the entries we have received. The imagination, energy and creativity which has gone into each young writer's entry made choosing the best poems a challenging and often difficult but ultimately hugely rewarding task - the general high standard of the work submitted amply vindicating this opportunity to bring their poetry to a larger appreciative audience.

We sincerely hope you are pleased with our final selection and that you will enjoy *Once Upon A Rhyme South Lancashire* for many years to come.

Contents

Madeleine Hughes (9) — 1

Abbey Village Primary School
Luke Townsend (11) — 1
Christopher Wrightson (11) — 1
Adam Barker (10) — 2
Anna Myerscough (10) — 2
Daniel Brown (11) — 2
Jessica Riley-Stuttard (8) — 2
John Norton (10) — 3
Megan Bywater (9) — 3
Lucy Clarkson (8) — 3
David Merry (9) — 3
Tarryn Hiller (8) — 4
Helen Whalley (9) — 4
Aimee Murphy (9) — 4
Amy Sturgess (9) — 5
Anya Townsend (7) — 5
Libby Burke (7) — 5
Charly Woodhead (7) — 6
Patrick Hughes (7) — 6
Alex Watson (8) — 6
Kelly Wrightson (9) — 7
Hayley Ratcliffe (9) — 7
Robert Girvin (8) — 7
Alistair Hodgson (8) — 8
Matthew Grey (9) — 8
Alex Bagwell (8) — 8
Tom Nolan (9) — 9
Glen Belcher (8) — 9
Harry Carson (9) — 9
Lily Crompton (9) — 10
Lucas Cradwell (10) — 10
William Manley (7) — 10
Nicholas Raymond (9) — 11
Madeleine Brown (9) — 11
Kate Burke (11) — 11
Stacey Tipping (10) — 12

Lauren Riley-Stuttard (10)   12
Sam Huxley-King (10)   12

Ashleigh Primary School
Freyja Gent (9)   13
Natalie Thirsk (8)   13
Liam Tabbinor (8)   13
Itrat Memon (7)   14
Thomas Chadwick (9)   14
Harry Campbell (8)   15
Charlie Greenwood (7)   15
Katie Donnelly (10)   16
Kate Forbes (7)   16
Adam Brogan (11)   17
Joshua Aspinall (8)   17
Holly Ballantyne (7)   18
Kelsey Parmar (8)   18
Lucy Atherton (10)   19
Emma Burt (8)   19
Shannon Waddicor (7)   20
Carl Fenwick (8)   20
Scarlett Taylor (7)   21
Joel Graves (9)   21
Gabrielle Hesmondhalgh (8)   22
Shannon Knowles (9)   22
Gregory Hughes (8)   22
Oliver Fradd (9)   23
Louis Kemp (8)   23
Mathew Forbes (8)   23
Abigail Kirwan (10)   24
Dylan Cooney (8)   24
Alyssia Walsh (10)   25
Ben Birkner (9)   25
Christopher Rowles (10)   26
Kelley Sharples (8)   26
Christopher Holden (9)   27
Liam Hargreaves (8)   27
Kieran McDermott (10)   28
Ashley Riding (8)   28
Emily Keys (10)   29
Abigail Alder (8)   29

Sadie Pilkington (9)	30
Jonathan Almond (9)	30
Adam Leigh (8)	30
Peter Huggill (9)	31
Joanne Mares (9)	31
Robert Foy (9)	31
Lucy Midgley (9)	32
Jordan Brown (9)	32
Charlotte Atkinson (10)	33
Daniel Hartley (10)	33
Liam Puzon (9)	34
Lucy King (9)	34
Liam Lonnen (8)	34
Adil Memon (9)	35
Joshua Lowry (10)	35
Jade Greenwood (9)	35
Laura Williams (8)	36
Ryan Doran (9)	36
Sara Black (9)	36
Conor Dawson (11)	37
Matthew Jennings (11)	37
Ben Ryder (9)	37
Jessica Nightingale (11)	38
Matthew Toplis (11)	39
Gemma Hulme (10)	39
Charlie Walsh (8)	39
Amy Atherton (10)	40
Natasha Hopwood (11)	40
Tori Brown (10)	41
Joshua Gent (11)	41
Rosie France (10)	42
Miles Starkie (11)	42
Lauren Berresford (10)	43
Jacob Hesmondhalgh (9)	43
Liam Birkner (11)	44
Lucy Starkie (11)	44
Jason Evans (10)	44
Maimuna Memon (11)	45
Lisa Proctor (10)	46
Matthew Lakey (9)	46

Avondale Primary School

Joe Bentley (11)	47
Sam Padbury (11)	47
Samantha Wright (6)	48
Jordan Astley (5)	48
Alex Worrall (5)	48
Carley Gaskell (10)	48
Hannah Brown (11)	49
Callum Evans (11)	49
Thurston Thomson (11)	50
Bryony Cookson	50
Amy Brogden (8)	51
Alice Brown (7)	51
Dean Riding (11)	52
Eve Middlehurst (9)	52
Charlotte Green (11)	53
Jaye Hecker (8)	53
Sam Smith (10)	54
Jack Thompson (9)	54
Stephen Malone (9)	55
Luke Atkinson (9)	55
Jade Whittaker (9)	56
Kayleigh Moir (9)	56
Sam Elliott (10)	57
Rebecca Brandon (10)	57
Billie Nesfield (9)	58
Michael Donnelly (9)	58
Cara-Beth Grimshaw (9)	58
Jack Hutchinson (9)	59
Grace Charlotte Jepson (8)	59
Jordan Walmsley (9)	59
Amy Earlam (9)	60
Tiffany Millsopp (10)	60
Lucy Morris (9)	61
Harley Pennington (10)	61
Liam Davis (9)	62
Rebekah Cardoo (9)	62
Bianca Mizon (10)	62
Rebecca Marsden (9)	63
Nicholas Holden (10)	63
Jack Sims (10)	63

Bradley Harper (10)	64
Jordan Taylor	64
Emma Marsden (9)	64
Emma Dudley (9)	65
Charlotte Grainger (9)	65
Katherine Byrne (10)	65
Nikki Henry	66
Jordan Kinsley-Smith (10)	66
Adam Lang (9)	66
Georgia Lennon (9)	67
Kyle Craven (9)	67
Zoe Charnock (10)	68
Zahira Mitha (9)	68
Jade Eaton (9)	69
Charlotte Tattersall (11)	69
Jack Mills (9)	70
Sophie Bannister (9)	70
Andrea Cooney (9)	70
Michael Clarke (9)	71
Chloe Brierley (9)	71
Amy Towers (9)	71
Faye Hutchinson (11)	72
Christopher Entwisle (11)	72
Kristan-Leigh Jennison (10)	73
Jessica Lewis (10)	73
Ryan Swanepoel (8)	74
Devon-Louise McKenna (9)	75
Matthew McKeown (9)	75
Adam Loonat (10)	76
Charlotte Rosson (11)	76
Anthony Ellis (11)	77
Lee Marsden (11)	77
Stephanie Cooke	78
Rebecca Bromley (9)	78
David Helmn (10)	79
Sophie Ashcroft (9)	79
Josie Bury (10)	80

Brinscall St John's CE Primary School

Alex Watson (10)	80
Matthew Parsons (10)	80

Georgina Hackett (9)	81
Nicole van der Linde (10)	81
Katie Rigby (9)	81
Grace Davies (10)	82
Kay Shuttleworth (10)	82
Isaac Worthington (10)	82
Ceri Yates (11)	83
Oliver Horrocks (9)	83
Hannah Kirkman (11)	84
Tobi Brown (11)	84
Madelyn Smith (10)	85
Freya Metters (10)	85
Harry Mullett (10)	86
Helen Savage (11)	86
Emily Burgoyne (10)	87
Grace Frost (10)	87
Robert Knowles (11)	88
Neil Parkinson (9)	88
Bethany Briggs (8)	89
Frederick Frost (9)	89
Elle Rossall (9)	90
Christopher Kirkman (9)	90
Josh Almond (11)	90
Nicola Green (8)	91
Alice Hume (9)	91
Charlotte Savage (9)	91
Oliver Yates (9)	92
Lewis Richardson (8)	92
Emily Yates (9)	92
Richard Ryding (9)	93
Jessica Taylor (8)	93
Rachael Wheeler (9)	93
Sally Booth (7)	94
Alice Powell (8)	94
Matthew Winterson (8)	94
Jacob Rose (7)	95
Jake Whitworth (7)	95
Olivia Day (7)	95
Georgina Ruffin (8)	96
Katie Ainscough (9)	96
Edward Dearden (7)	97
Alicia Howarth (7)	97

Christopher Parkinson (7)	98
Matthew van der Linde (8)	98
Bradley Hardy (8)	99
Jac Vincent (8)	99
Rachel Stringfellow (8)	100

Burscough Village Primary School

Martyn McLean (9)	100
Jonathan McDonald (10)	101
Kerris Halsall (10)	102
Christopher May (9)	103
Daniel Caunce (9)	104
Rachel Prescott (10)	105
Jake Spencer (10)	106
Kim Burke (10)	107
Emma Francis (10)	108
Danielle Keogan (10)	109
Daniel Santos (11)	110
Megan Elloy (10)	111
Sean Kelly (10)	112
Alan Mawdsley (10)	113
Rebecca Power (10)	114
Phillip King (11)	115
Michael Boucher (11)	116
Christopher Rice (11)	117
Christina Martland (10)	118
Simon Clegg (10)	119
Kieran Forshaw (11)	120
Kurtis Rothwell (9)	121
Christopher Watson (11)	122

Christ Church CE School

Sam Bowker (11)	122
Eleanor White (11)	123
Olivia Laycock (10)	123
Megan Cox (11)	124
Ainsley Roscoo (10)	124
Lauren Ingram (11)	124
Siôn Wells (11)	124
Harriet Rigby (10)	125
Jonathan Frost (11)	125

Mason Banks (10)	125
Sam Richardson (10)	125
Eleanor Attwood-Jones (10)	126
Lucy Dawson (11)	126
Louie Turner (10)	126
Sam Lacey (11)	127
Jordan Simpson (10)	127
Gemma Bowers (10)	127
Emily Potter (10)	128
Jack Dalby (10)	128

Gilded Hollins Primary School

Paul Lowcock (8)	129
Adam Purcell (8)	129
Annabelle Harrison (9)	130
James Hodgson (9)	130
Thomas Hibbert (9)	131
Adam Pierce Jones (10)	131
Anya Hoque (10)	132
Joseph Heaton (10)	132
Joshua Wilcock (9)	133
Daniel Mason (9)	133
Daniel Wood (9)	134
Jareth Turner (10)	134
Matthew Royle (9)	135
Bethany Bramall (9)	135
Milo Pendlebury (9)	136
Emma Seddon (10)	136
Jessica Bolton (10)	137
Rosie Willis (10)	137
Alex Miller (10)	138
Lucy Woodcock (9)	138
Nicola Goulden (10)	139
Alexandra Larkin (10)	139
Sally Boardman (11)	140
Alex Cordery (10)	140
Adam King (11)	141
Georgia Overend (10)	141
Daniel Lynch (10)	142
Daniel Kidd (11)	142
Amy Wilcock (10)	143

Charlotte Monaghan (10) 143
Thomas Walsh (11) 144
Sam Blower (11) 144

Lordsgate Township CE Primary School
Hannah Rothwell (8) 145
Naomi Maher (9) 145
Eleanor McCombe (9) 146
Elliott Howarth (8) 146
Jessica Walsh (8) 147
Aaron Kendall (9) 147
Rebecca Pickering (9) 148
Sean Smith (9) 148
Steven Dawson (9) 149
Bethany Graves (10) 149
Danielle Hayman (7) 149

Roby Mill CE Primary School
Kathryn Bridgeman (10) 150
Isaac Bradley (9) 150
Jordan Scully (11) 150
Josceline Halsall (10) 151
Nicola Bradley (9) 151
Laura Burton (11) 151
Tom Aitchison (9) 152
Melissa Hale (9) 152
James Carrington (9) 152
Eleanor Swire (11) 153
Rachel Appleton (8) 153
Jasmine Turner (8) 154
Winston Halsall (7) 154
Drew Winstanley (8) 154
Patrick Green (11) 154
Camilla Turner (11) 155
Laura Swire (8) 155

St Hugh's CE Primary School, Oldham
Martina Kiernan (11) 155
Frank Ross (10) 156
Jordan Senior (10) 156

Kieron Bland (10)	156
Chloe Clarke (9)	157
Laura Worrall (11)	157
Charlotte Marsden (11)	157
Jessica Bird (10)	158
Daniel Lord (9)	158
Sarah Ryder (8)	159
Michael Doyle (11)	159
Liam Welsh (9)	160
Rebecca Bird (8)	160
Andrew Lomas (8)	160
Natalie Wardle (8)	161
Emma Henderson (8)	161
Ashley Stewart (8)	161
Candice Jones (10)	162
Rebecca Holland (8)	163
Bethany Shackleton (10)	163
Rebecca Cooper (8)	164
Brandon Clifton (8)	164

St James' CE Primary School, Chorley

Gabrielle Miller-Crook (10)	165
Philip Jolly (10)	165
Eleanor Hargreaves (11)	166
Vicky Charnley (10)	166
Jake Sloan (10)	167
Olivia Facer (10)	167
Joanna Price (9)	168
Katie Parker (11)	168

St John's CE Primary School, Burscough

Jessica Edwards (9)	169
Emma Aldred (9)	169
Laura Wilkinson (10)	170
Adam Nelson (10)	170
Melissa Jones (9)	171
Isabel Bryant (8)	171
Zoe Davies (9)	172
Helena Jamieson (9)	172
Rebecca Griggs (9)	173
Zoe Winders (9)	173

Joanna Lowe (9)	174
Sarah Woods (9)	174
Rebecca Moseley (9)	175
Annie McLoughlin (10)	175
Sally Wade (9)	176
Kayleigh Sutherland (10)	177
James Powell (10)	178
Rosie Burrell (10)	178

St Mark's CE Primary School, Scarisbrick
Samantha Lee (9)	179
Megan Claeys-Sheridan (10)	179
Holly Jackson (10)	180
Tanya Steele (10)	180
Nicola Ball (10)	180

St Mary's CE Primary School, Greenfield
Jonathan Rhodes (10)	181
Evie Maxwell (9)	181
Beth Cavanagh (10)	182
Natalie Mallalieu (10)	182
Daniela Soldner (10)	183
Amelia Fenlon (9)	183
Lewis Ralph (8)	184
Christopher Shawmarsh-Smith (8)	184
Andrew Marsden (10)	185
Adam Smalley (10)	185
Hannah Claydon (7)	186
Thomas Woolley (9)	186
Faith Stanford (10)	187
Joel Stanton (9)	187
Emma Stagg (10)	188
Cameron Maxwell (10)	188
James Moore (10)	189
Benjamin Rothery (9)	190
Katie Gartside (9)	190
Sophie Kemp (10)	191
Rebecca Childs (11)	191
Christian Shoel (9)	191
Jonathan Beilby (9)	192
David Lyons (11)	192

Sophie Paterson (9) — 193
Robert Edwards (11) — 193
Jessica Shaw (10) — 194
Natalie Burgess (10) — 194
Rebecca Bell (11) — 195
Andrew Walford (9) — 195
Lawrence Copson (11) — 196
Gemma Barlow (10) — 196
Bethany Kippax (11) — 196
Hayley Lockeridge (11) — 197
Megan Fahy (7) — 197
May Wall (8) — 197
Elizabeth Shoel (11) — 198
Amy Winterbottom (10) — 198
Benjamin Hall (11) — 199
Eleanor Butterworth (8) — 199
Toby Jones (8) — 200
Nina Jones (10) — 200
James Wright (8) — 201

St Peter's CE Junior School, Leigh
Zoe Molyneux (9) — 201
Christopher Hamer (9) — 202
Chloe McDonough (9) — 202
Becky Abbott (9) — 202
Laura Balmer (9) — 203
Lauren Ashbrook (8) — 203
Justin Burns (9) — 203
Sarah Dean (9) — 204
Bryoni Parkinson (9) — 204
Kimberly Blackburn (9) — 205

Withnell Fold Primary School
Deborah Norris (9) — 205
Nikki Evans (11) — 206
Chelsea Waterhouse (9) — 206
Danielle Jackson (10) — 207
Luke Davy (11) — 207
Charlie Patterson (10) — 208
James Hopkin (10) — 209
Elizabeth Jones (10) — 209

Edward Melling (10)   210
Allan Struthers (10)   210
Maria Peck (11)   211
Alexander Snape (9)   211
Shona Jackson (9)   212

The Poems

Spring's Call

Baby lamb's first cry
As it opens its eye.
First flower grows
As the rooster crows.
Sun shines high,
In the bright sky.
This is what the spring
Will always bring!

Madeleine Hughes (9)

Kennings

Brown gold
Always sold
Loved by all
Large and small
Bitter and sweet
What a treat
Drunk cold and hot
Hits the spot.

A - Chocolate.

Luke Townsend (11)
Abbey Village Primary School

Kennings

Penny nicker
Alarm setter offer
Glass breaker
Treasure taker
Face hider
Soon it will all have gone.

A - Burglar.

Christopher Wrightson (11)
Abbey Village Primary School

Limerick

There once was a parrot from Wales
Who wanted to eat some French snails
He got in a plane
But it crashed on a crane
And then he ended up with no tails.

Adam Barker (10)
Abbey Village Primary School

Limerick

There once was a woman from Chorley,
Who one day became very poorly,
She sat down to cry,
And said, 'I'm gonna die'
Because her head hurt very sorely.

Anna Myerscough (10)
Abbey Village Primary School

The Man From The Moon

There once was a man from the moon
Who had never seen a spoon
He went to New York
But he only saw forks
So he said, 'I'm watching cartoons.'

Daniel Brown (11)
Abbey Village Primary School

Hate

It tastes all bitter and people hate me
It smells like musty frog snails
It looks like I have ragged clothes
It sounds like dragging footsteps.

Jessica Riley-Stuttard (8)
Abbey Village Primary School

Lotuses

Lotuses are good
They are very fast but old
They are wicked cars
They have convertible roofs
They can travel really fast.

John Norton (10)
Abbey Village Primary School

Loneliness

Loneliness is dark brown like a tree trunk,
It smells like rotten cheese,
It tastes like sour raindrops,
It feels like you're locked away,
It sounds like the flood of tears.

Megan Bywater (9)
Abbey Village Primary School

Fear

Fear is like a dark black cloud
It tastes like bitter lemon
And smells strong
It looks mean.

Lucy Clarkson (8)
Abbey Village Primary School

Love

It tastes like butterflies
It smells like flowers
It looks like a rainbow
It sounds like giggling
It feels nice.

David Merry (9)
Abbey Village Primary School

Happiness

Happiness is as orange as the bright summer sun
It tastes like strawberries and cream
It smells like blossom
It looks like a sea of smiling faces
It sounds like the happy sounds of the funfair
It feels like you've got the biggest smile in the world.

Tarryn Hiller (8)
Abbey Village Primary School

Anger

Anger is red and orange like a blazing fire
It tastes like red-hot chillies
It smells like a horrible rotten egg
It looks like a tall bonfire
It sounds like terrible shouting
It feels like you're locked inside yourself.

Helen Whalley (9)
Abbey Village Primary School

Anger

Anger is navy-blue
It tastes like sour lemon
It smells like dead flowers
It looks like a dismal day
It sounds like mad shouting
It feels like you're in a cage.

Aimee Murphy (9)
Abbey Village Primary School

Happiness

Happiness is bright red like the sun
It tastes like warm sweets
It smells warm and tasty
It looks like a warm sun
It sounds like soft footsteps
It feels like a soft cushion.

Amy Sturgess (9)
Abbey Village Primary School

Fear

Fear is black and scary

It tastes like mud

It smells like green cheese

It looks like a dark house

It sounds like a ghost

It feels like there is no one beside you.

Anya Townsend (7)
Abbey Village Primary School

Jealousy

It sounds like a deep hole
It feels like danger
Jealousy is dark purple like a gloomy room
It tastes like bugs
It smells like a dustbin
It looks like an empty house.

Libby Burke (7)
Abbey Village Primary School

Happiness

It feels like fun
Happiness is yellow like a flower
It tastes like hot chocolate
It smells sweet
It looks excellent
It sounds like laughter and joy.

Charly Woodhead (7)
Abbey Village Primary School

Happiness

Happiness is yellow like the sun
It tastes like chilli
It smells like hot chocolate
It looks like a lit street
It sounds like flying flowers
It feels like being together.

Patrick Hughes (7)
Abbey Village Primary School

Happiness

It tastes like jam
It feels hot
It sounds like singing
It smells like smelly socks
It looks very nice
It feels frightened.

Alex Watson (8)
Abbey Village Primary School

Fear!

Fear is very scary,
And is not as gentle as a fairy.
Scary is like footsteps following you,
Spooky, shhh, spooky,
It feels like you're all alone,
That's what fear is.

Kelly Wrightson (9)
Abbey Village Primary School

Happiness

Happiness is a lovely castle
It tastes like ice cream
It smells like berry ice cream
It looks like a lovely castle with some ice cream
It sounds like it is horrible
It feels like I am at home.

Hayley Ratcliffe (9)
Abbey Village Primary School

Fear

Fear is black like part of space
It tastes like mouldy toast
It smells like burning toast
It looks like a black road
It sounds like footsteps
It feels like wet stone.

Robert Girvin (8)
Abbey Village Primary School

Anger

Anger is black like a dark gloomy cave
It tastes like a cold misty day
It smells dusty and dry
It looks like a ball of fire
It sounds like a powerful shotgun
It feels like a hot flame.

Alistair Hodgson (8)
Abbey Village Primary School

Happiness

Happiness is bright colours mixed together
It tastes like a nice mug of hot chocolate
It smells warm and soft and loving
It looks like Heaven
It sounds like the birds singing
It feels like being in a magical world.

Matthew Grey (9)
Abbey Village Primary School

Happiness

Happiness is like the sun
It tastes like a flora
It smells fresh
It looks like people smiling
It sounds like the waves
It feels like fun.

Alex Bagwell (8)
Abbey Village Primary School

Love

Love is like a locked up drawer
It tastes like beautiful flowers
It smells like blossom
It looks like the beautiful colours of flowers
It sounds like the noises of nature
It feels like a really soft cushion.

Tom Nolan (9)
Abbey Village Primary School

Anger

Anger is dark grey like a mossy brick
It smells like blood
It tastes like rust
It looks like dust
It sounds like glass
It feels like the wind with a temper.

Glen Belcher (8)
Abbey Village Primary School

Fear

Fear is when you are in a room where no candles are lit
It tastes like mouldy bread
It smells like a dead rat
It looks like a pitch-black room
It's like you are alone.

Harry Carson (9)
Abbey Village Primary School

Kennings

Nut cracker
Hibernation maker
Rusty crawler
Tree swinger
Conker stealer
Bird frightener.

A - Squirrel.

Lily Crompton (9)
Abbey Village Primary School

Untitled

Everyone knows it's very sweet
Tastes a lot better than your grandpa's feet
All the other drinks this will beat
Screw off the lid
And take a sip
Let it go down your throat with a drip.

A - Coke.

Lucas Gradwell (10)
Abbey Village Primary School

Love

It tastes like strawberries
It smells like a red flower
It looks like fun
It sounds like fun
It feels like happiness.

William Manley (7)
Abbey Village Primary School

The Woolly Jumper

Body warmer
Stops cold trauma
Full of heat
Sometimes a birthday treat
Different shapes and sizes
The French say 'Can I try zis?'

A - A jumper.

Nicholas Raymond (9)
Abbey Village Primary School

Kennings

Picture flicker
Remote clicker
Screen watcher
Full of laughter
Different programmes
For different ages.

A - TV.

Madeleine Brown (9)
Abbey Village Primary School

Pirates' Plunder

Pirates' plunder
Locked-up wonder
Secret holder
Gleaming boulder
Sandy layer
Lost forever.

A - Treasure chest.

Kate Burke (11)
Abbey Village Primary School

Kennings About Javine

Pitch singer
Hit movie maker
Beyoncé lookalike
Self singer
Non rocker
Smooth beater
CD buster
Jeans lover
Non skirt wearer
Groovy dancer
She was in the last six for Girls Aloud
Singer of 'Real Things'.

A - Javine.

Stacey Tipping (10)
Abbey Village Primary School

Limerick

There once was a man from Chorley
The doctor said he was poorly
He felt very sick
So he had to leave quick
But got better slowly but surely.

Lauren Riley-Stuttard (10)
Abbey Village Primary School

Limerick

There once was an old man from Peru
Who desperately needed the loo
He looked high and low
For somewhere to go
'I hate this weird place in Peru.'

Sam Huxley-King (10)
Abbey Village Primary School

Isobel

Isobel met a skinny green witch
Isobel, Isobel didn't snitch
The witch was skinny, the witch was mean
The witch was tiny, the witch was green.
Glad to meet you witch, now I will make you scream.
Isobel, Isobel didn't worry.
Isobel didn't scream or scurry
She brushed her hair and gave her a big scare
Then the skinny green witch went out in a twitch.

Freyja Gent (9)
Ashleigh Primary School

My Bedroom

My bedroom is a tip
It looks a dump
When my mum goes in
I hear her scream.

A stinky old teddy
Gazing at the wall
My bedroom is a tip.

Natalie Thirsk (8)
Ashleigh Primary School

Haiku - A Fish

My fish is crazy
It swims fast around the tank
My fish is crazy.

Liam Tabbinor (8)
Ashleigh Primary School

My Bedroom Is A Tip

My bedroom is a tip
It is very scary
It is like a skip
It couldn't fit a fairy.

It is very rusty
It is very old
It is very dusty
It is full of mould.

It is very creepy
It's like a dump
I'm never sleepy
Because it makes me jump.

Rusty cars, orange crumbs
And K'Nex galore.
Taped plastic swords
I think I'm going to get squashed to the floor.

Itrat Memon (7)
Ashleigh Primary School

The Falcon

The falcon is like a massive jet
Flying in the air.
Its wings are spread out like
Hovering bees gliding in the air.
It's like a hungry predator, darting
Down at its prey with its beak.
Its eyes are evil like the Devil's eyes.
In the air it starts screeching like a
Hungry, starving dinosaur.

Thomas Chadwick (9)
Ashleigh Primary School

My Bedroom

My bedroom is a tip
It looks like a skip!
A terrifying dump
It makes me jump.

Lots of things scattered all over the place,
But my mum says it's a disgrace.
My ripped teddy on the floor
My mum bangs on the door.

There are mice
My mum says it's not very nice
My pets do not go near
No wonder they fear.

Harry Campbell (8)
Ashleigh Primary School

My Bedroom

My bedroom is a tip
It's a real mess
I wish it was tidy
Why does it have to be messy?

It's got make-up on the floor
And a colourful wind charm making lots of noise
A smelly T-shirt smelling away on the floor
And a broken old plug lying on the floor.

My bedroom is a tip
It's a real mess
I wish it was tidy
Why does it have to be messy?

Charlie Greenwood (7)
Ashleigh Primary School

My Penfriend

Me and my penfriend
Were friends since we were little.
We went to playschool together,
Never, never did we squabble,
And then came the day
My penfriend went away.

Me and my penfriend
Were friends since we were little.
We went to school together,
Played always together,
And then came the day
My penfriend went away.

Me and my penfriend
Were friends since we were little.
We grew older and older,
But still we were together
And then came the day,
My penfriend went away.

Katie Donnelly (10)
Ashleigh Primary School

My Bedroom

My bedroom is untidy, my bedroom is a disgrace.
My toys think it is good to have a little race.
My bedroom is a tip, it looks like a skip.
My dirty teddy walks round the room.

The chewy sweets make people's feet stick to the floor.
My rag doll thinks deep thoughts.
My colourful yo-yo walks round the room.
My crisp packet crumbles on the floor.

Kate Forbes (7)
Ashleigh Primary School

Sports Mayhem

Ball bouncer
Net shooter
Huge jammer
Great hammer
Super jumper
Excellent slam-dunker
Outstanding runner
Six-foot body
Healthy eater
Baseline cheater
Sweaty player
Great lay upper
Goal tender
Ball sender
Net jammer
Ball hanger.

Adam Brogan (11)
Ashleigh Primary School

Fireworks

The time is here
The sun has gone down
There's a strange sound
The sky is sparkling with glory.

Boom! Boom!

Burning for his life
The fire blazing
Growing like a flower.

Joshua Aspinall (8)
Ashleigh Primary School

My Bedroom

My bedroom is a tip
There's nowhere you can stand
Sometimes you can slip because of my glittery
Multicoloured make-up.

You have to push the door
And then you slip because
Of my brown slippy banana skin
And a raggy holey top.

Sometimes you have to jump
Over my toys and sometimes
You nearly trip over my ripped books
And my old bear.

Holly Ballantyne (7)
Ashleigh Primary School

My Bedroom

My bedroom is a tip
It looks like a skip!
A terrifying dump
It makes me jump!

It looks like a disgrace
My mum says 'Put your things in their place.'
Everything is scattered all over the place.
So I put everything in its place.

I put the dirty teddy on the bed
Gazing at the wall.

Kelsey Parmar (8)
Ashleigh Primary School

Guess Who?

Fast runner
Cute cuddler
Fur tickler
Body scratcher
Tail wagger
Fun player
Slow eater
Bed sleeper
Angry biter
Door outer
Biscuit watcher
Hand licker
Loud barker
Toy fetcher
People liker
Bobble hater
Animal finder
Hurt helper.

Lucy Atherton (10)
Ashleigh Primary School

My Bedroom

My bedroom is a tip
It is a disgrace
My mum calls it a dump
Everything has a place!

My dad calls it a junkyard
It is so messy
But that is how I like it
My mum goes absolutely stressy.

Emma Burt (8)
Ashleigh Primary School

My Bedroom

My bedroom is a tip
It looks like a skip!
It's just a big lump
I can't get into it.

There's a black slippy banana skin,
Just dumped on the floor.
My mum just
Can't take anymore.

A horrible patch,
Of makeup on the floor.

Shannon Waddicor (7)
Ashleigh Primary School

My Bedroom

My bedroom is a tip
It looks like a disgrace
It makes me jump
Like a fish in the sea.

My bedroom is a tip
My mum says it stinks
With ripped soggy plates
Playing dead on the floor.

My bedroom is a tip
With an old rusty TV that doesn't even work.

Carl Fenwick (8)
Ashleigh Primary School

Listen

Silence is when you can hear things
Listen

A slimy worm crawling through the fresh
Green grass.

Eyelids beautifully closing when I go to sleep.

A gentle breathing of a buzzy bee.

A moth's footsteps jumping very, very quickly
On the grey path.

A black spider racing round the silver sink.

Scarlett Taylor (7)
Ashleigh Primary School

The Weather

The lightning is like a bright yellow fish
jumping from the sky.
The sun is like a golden hamster
curled up in a ball.
The snow is like a white bumpy yeti
on the ground.
The hail is like thousands of tiny birds
pecking very fast.
The wind is like a giant dog
sneezing.
The earthquakes are like a stampede of elephants.

Joel Graves (9)
Ashleigh Primary School

My Bedroom

My bedroom is a messy place
My mum says there are mushy peas
Spreading gravy all over the floor
And a paralysing teddy bear
Gazing up to space.

She says there are run out Game Boys
Spreading batteries all over the floor
And rusty sharp darts chucked at the wall.

Gabrielle Hesmondhalgh (8)
Ashleigh Primary School

The Weather

The snow is like a beautiful white butterfly
The lightning is like a snake sticking its tongue out.
The rain is like an ant floating through the sky.
The wind is like an elephant blowing its trunk.
The sun is like a peacock flying in the sky.
Hailstones are like a tiny but heavy hippo.
The sky is like a pile of us with blue shirts and white shirts.

Shannon Knowles (9)
Ashleigh Primary School

Listen

Silence is when you can hear things listen . . .

The stars in the sky moving
A wriggly pink worm walking in the tiny grass
When you go to sleep you close your eyelids
An ant walking in soil
A moth's footfall.

Gregory Hughes (8)
Ashleigh Primary School

The Weather

A rainbow is like a colourful peacock.
Thunder is like a stamping elephant.
Lightning is like a flashing falcon.
The wind is like a swooping eagle.
Hailstones are like a fast rhinoceros.
Snow is like a slushy owl.
The rain is like a drenched kangaroo.

Oliver Fradd (9)
Ashleigh Primary School

The Weather

A rainbow is like a bright, colourful peacock.
The thunder is like a yellow flying snake.
The wind is like a howling owl.
The rain is like the white milk from a cow.
The sun is like a golden tortoise in its shell.
The snow is like some of the smooth skin from a polar bear.
The lightning is like a flashing fish.

Louis Kemp (8)
Ashleigh Primary School

The Weather

The rainbow is like a colourful parrot.
The thunderstorm is like an incredible eagle swooping down.
The wind is like a massive wave.
The hail is like a fast penguin.
The lightning is like an electric seal.
The sun is like a golden falcon.
The rain is like the sea through a bumpy wave.

Mathew Forbes (8)
Ashleigh Primary School

Excuses, Excuses

Why are you late Calvey?
Cow ate my uniform Sir.
What about yesterday then?
Lost my head Sir.
Lost your head?
Went crazy Sir.
What about the day before that?
My grandma was at Weightwatchers
trying to lose weight Sir.
And this has all been on maths test days?
Well it's very, very weird, but my dad keeps on
losing his pants Sir.
Why Calvey?
Don't know Sir.
I asked you a question, Calvey!
Did you? What was it then?
I said why did your dad keep losing his pants?
What about last week Calvey?
Oh my car blew up Sir!
Oh, I've had enough of this, go and sit down in your place.

Abigail Kirwan (10)
Ashleigh Primary School

The Weather

The thunder is like an elephant.
The sun is like a bright golden bird.
The tornado is like a dog.
The hurricane is like a wolf.
The wind is like a flying duck.

Dylan Cooney (8)
Ashleigh Primary School

Please Mum

Small horse, big horse,
Old horse, young horse
Big ball of mud horse
Guaranteed long life horse
Too hard to ride horse
No fun at all horse
I hate the water horse
Up on the moors horse
Waterproof and heatproof horse
Hold on very tight horse
Don't jump the jump horse
Who would want this horse?
Definitely this horse
Wow look at that horse!
Prefer that one over there horse
It has to be that horse
Not my cup of tea horse
I got it free horse
Look at the price tag horse
Cost a lotta money horse
Please Mum, get me a horse!

Alyssia Walsh (10)
Ashleigh Primary School

The Weather

A lightning storm is like a raging lion
The sun is like a golden, curled up hedgehog in the sky.
The wind is like a swooping swallow.
Hailstone is like a squirrel falling with speed.
Thunder is like a rhinoceros stomping in the distance.
Rain is like soggy, falling flies.
A hurricane is like a super strong gorilla
Blowing hard on the Earth.

Ben Birkner (9)
Ashleigh Primary School

The Friend Alphabet

A is for Alex, who is good at football.
B is for Ben, who can run up a wall.
C is for Charlie, the one with big feet.
D is for Danny, I think he is really neat.
E is for Elliot, with the 30cm smile.
F is for friends, they're really worthwhile.
G is for Garry, who has got a BB gun.
H is for Henry, he likes having fun.
I is for Ian, who thinks he invented the medieval rack.
J is for Jack, if you don't be careful, he will give you a whack.
K is for Keiran, he has got lots of slime.
L is for Liam, who has committed a crime.
M is for Michel, his favourite colour is red.
N is for Neil, he usually stays in bed.
O is for Owen, I think he lives in a shell.
P is for Phil, he has been locked in a cell.
Q is for Q, he thinks he is from James Bond.
R is for Rob, who owns a pond.
S is for Simon, who really likes the snow.
T is for Ted, who is always on the go.
U is for Uka, who comes from Africa.
V is for Vince, who is always shouting, *'Eureka!'*
W is for William, who always breaks glass.
X is for Xavier, his plane trips are always first class.
Y is for Yogi, his name sounds like a bear's.
Z is for Zog, who comes from a planet made of pears!

Christopher Rowles (10)
Ashleigh Primary School

The Weather

The wind is like a gliding dolphin
The snow is like a pure polar bear
The lightning is like an electric eel
The tornado is like a whizzing fish
The sun is like a ginger squirrel.

Kelley Sharples (8)
Ashleigh Primary School

Excuses, Excuses

Where's your homework, Holden?
House blew up Sir.
And why was your dad late for parents' evening?
Dad's feet turned into jetpacks Sir.
So, where is your pencil boy?
The dog ate my pencil Sir.
Right then, time for tennis practice then!
Can't Sir.
There's no such word as 'can't'!
Ripped bat Sir.
Then couldn't you have bought a new one then?
No Sir.
Why?
No change Sir.
Get some from your mum then.
Can't Sir.
Why?
Mum shrunk Sir.
Well what about your grandma then?
Sorry Sir.
Why?
Grandma's hands blew off Sir.
Well what about your grandad?
Dead Sir.
Holden, all your family are weird, so you are excused.

Christopher Holden (9)
Ashleigh Primary School

The Weather

The snow is a soft tiger.
The wind is a flying cow.
The lightning is a fast bird.
The rain is a loud elephant.
The sun is a shining snake.
The fog is a muddy pig.

Liam Hargreaves (8)
Ashleigh Primary School

Crocodile

People eater
Never sleeper
Tail user
Lake cruiser
Catfish creeper
Water leaper
Tail slapper
Mouth snapper
Man struggler
Fish juggler
Sly grinner
Water dimmer
Ground slider
Green slimer
Children scarer
Baby carer
Beaver chaser
Dam breaker
Awful singer
Green finger
Smelly pongs
Even longer than a conga!

Kieran McDermott (10)
Ashleigh Primary School

Haiku - A Fish

They do slip a lot
They swim a lot all day long
They are very small.

Ashley Riding (8)
Ashleigh Primary School

My Friend!

My friend is very silly
Her nickname is Silly Billy
She wriggles at night
But she doesn't bite
She makes it sunny
She's always funny
She loves to sing
She loves nice things
She loves to lark about
She always yells and shouts
She loves to play with dogs
She's not fond of frogs
She's always got a smile on her face
She's always in the right place
She's never mean
She's always keen
   And that's my friend!
   Do you have one?

Emily Keys (10)
Ashleigh Primary School

The Weather

The lightning is like an electric eel.
The snow is as white as a swan.
The sun is like a ginger lion.
The fog is like a small squirrel.
The thunder is like a lion roaring.
The hurricane is like an orang-utan swinging
Through the tree.

Abigail Alder (8)
Ashleigh Primary School

The Weather

The lightning is like dark-coloured snakes shooting from the sky.
The wind is like a gliding sea horse.
The snow is like a noisy polar bear.
An earthquake is like a shark going mad after a fish.
Hailstones are like nasty spiders
Jumping on you.

Sadie Pilkington (9)
Ashleigh Primary School

The Weather

The snow is like a soft tiger.
The sun is like a golden bird.
The rain is like a splashing whale.
An earthquake is like an octopus,
Getting dropped from the clouds.
The wind is like a bird flapping in your face.
The lightning is like a hare running.
The thunder is like an electric eel.

Jonathan Almond (9)
Ashleigh Primary School

The Weather

The snow is a trampling polar bear.
The raincloud is a nice snow fox.
The rain is like a wet flying fish.
The lightning is a bright yellow bird.
The sun is a golden fish.
The wind is a beautiful rabbit.

Adam Leigh (8)
Ashleigh Primary School

Isabel

Isabel met a witch,
Isabel, Isabel didn't twitch.
The witch was called Mary
And the witch was very scary.
The witch said hello,
Then the witch played her cello.
Isabel, Isabel, didn't worry,
Isabel didn't scream or scurry,
Then Isabel said she was going to cast
                         a spell on her
And she did.

Peter Huggill (9)
Ashleigh Primary School

The Weather

The sun is like a golden duck.
The lightning is like a grass snake.
A hailstone is like a fast rabbit.
The wind is a flying fish.
The thunder is like a budgie.
Snow is like a guinea pig.
The tornado is like a bull.

Joanne Mares (9)
Ashleigh Primary School

Haiku - A Fish

A fish is orange
Fish like to be in water
Fish like the water.

Robert Foy (9)
Ashleigh Primary School

My Auntie

My auntie smells of perfume, the kind that makes you sneeze!
And if you smell the bottle,
It makes you cough and wheeze.
She has a box of chocolates, she keeps in a biscuit tin,
And if we're really, really good,
She lets us peep right in!
But if we're bad, oh woe betide,
She shuts the lid and snaps your nose inside!
Of all the aunties I could have had,
I got landed with this type.
One that didn't smell of perfume, and didn't make us eat tripe!
But she is alright really, I sort of suppose,
As long as we're not bad, because we get a sore nose!

Lucy Midgley (9)
Ashleigh Primary School

The Weather

The wind is like a fluttering bird.
The lightning is like an electric eel.
The hailstone is like a tiny noisy polar bear.
The sun is like a whirling golden bird.
The rain is like a horrible cold shower.
The thunder is like a lion roaring.
The snow is like a frozen dove.
The night sky is like a black pit.
The stars are like little night lights.
An earthquake is like a curled up snake.
The space is like a smooth coat on a horse.
The waves are like a coat on a sheep.

Jordan Brown (9)
Ashleigh Primary School

My Family Tree

This is a poem about my family tree
Apart from the fact that it's written by me.
Let's start from the top,
Now there's Grandma Pop.
There's my great auntie Sue who's married to Drew.
Then there's cousin Harry and Uncle Barry.
There's Auntie Cath who lived in Bath.
Down south there's cousin Ralth,
Who owns a strawberry farm.
Then there's Uncle Marn and Auntie Barn.
Then there's my mother and father
We all live in Gather
When it comes to me I'm at the end
I wished my family lived round the bend.

Charlotte Atkinson (10)
Ashleigh Primary School

Christopher

Chris is a caring and truthful friend,
He helps me when I get offended,
Often he reminds me to go for my dinner!
He gives me support, he's a real good sport,
Chris is such a good friend.

Chris is funny, even funnier than a bunny,
He can hit people with footballs,
But when we fall out, we make up, laugh and joke!
He gives me support, he's a real good sport,
Chris is such a funny friend.

Daniel Hartley (10)
Ashleigh Primary School

The Eagle

He sets his eyes
on his prey,
as accurate as laser beams.
Then he darts,
after his prey,
heading for bullseye.
He messes with his meals,
before eating.
The eagle
never, ever misses.

Liam Puzon (9)
Ashleigh Primary School

The Snail

Slimy snail
Wriggling all around
Slimy snail
Leaving lots of slime
Slimy snail
Slowly moves around
Slimy snail.

Lucy King (9)
Ashleigh Primary School

Haiku - The Tiger

Tigers have got stripes
Tigers have fat, fluffy claws
Tigers have big fangs.

Liam Lonnen (8)
Ashleigh Primary School

Kangaroo

The kangaroo has soft silky golden fur
It is like a jack-in-a-box while it jumps so high,
It's like it jumps over the moon,
The kangaroo speeds as fast as a motor car,
Its non-stop engine goes on and on
Till it rests and lies down.
A fluffy brown tummy and
A small mischievous face
Makes the kangaroo look so innocent.

Adil Memon (9)
Ashleigh Primary School

The Skyscraper

The skyscraper is big
But thin as a twig.
It is very tall
And makes everything look small.
It has lots of windows
Which look like lots of eyes.

Joshua Lowry (10)
Ashleigh Primary School

The White Tiger

The white tiger is . . .
Like a polar bear with black stripes,
Camouflaged fur in the Arctic,
A tongue as red as a pool of blood,
Sounds a bit like maracas and drums
That is what the white tiger is.

Jade Greenwood (9)
Ashleigh Primary School

The Weather

The wind is like a dog panting loudly.
The sun is like a golden koala.
The snow is like a white spider.
The lightning is like a dog barking madly.
The hailstones are like tiny butterflies.
The rain is like a massive whale squirting water.
The fog is like a grey monkey covering up the sun.
The earthquake is like the long legs of an octopus
Going round and round.
The clouds are like sheep in the sky.
A rainbow is like a multicoloured parrot.

Laura Williams (8)
Ashleigh Primary School

The Weather

The sun is like a golden eagle
The snow is like a fierce polar bear
The lightning is like a yellow, loud and scary lion's tail,
The wind is like lots of trees,
A tornado is like a dog chasing its tail.

Ryan Doran (9)
Ashleigh Primary School

The Weather

The wind is like a grey hippopotamus
The sun is like a yellow hawk
The lightning is like a slithering lizard
The hailstone is like a white polar bear
The snow is like a snowy owl.

Sara Black (9)
Ashleigh Primary School

The Jobberwocky

One, two! One, two!
To battle and to battle.
The deadly sword went crock-snap!
He left it dead and with its head went galloping back.

It was brilliant
And the slimy toads sang and danced in the wind.
All happy were the people
And the Jobberwocky growled.

Conor Dawson (11)
Ashleigh Primary School

Digger

Grave digger
Garden sorter
Soil mover
Hole maker
Brick lifter
Rubbish sorter
Metal reporter
Digger.

Matthew Jennings (11)
Ashleigh Primary School

Haiku - A Fish

Orange fish swimming
The fish is really greedy
The fish has brown spots.

Ben Ryder (9)
Ashleigh Primary School

My Brother!

Nose picker
Toe flicker
Useless walker
Cute talker
Video seer
Nappy weer
Mess maker
Time taker
Family waker
Rattle shaker
Ball kicker
Second ticker
Silent creeper
Not a sleeper
Sofa peeper
Sleeping deeper
Hand clapper
Sister slapper
Mother cuddler
Room muddler
Sloppy kisser
Cheek misser
Toy hitter
Knee sitter
Night howler
Secret prowler
Food gobbler
Little toddler
Loves his mother
My brother!

Jessica Nightingale (11)
Ashleigh Primary School

Budgie

Football screecher
Hoover liker
Budgie lover
Cat hater
Getting older
Seed eater
Water drinker
Finger nipper
Flying higher
Lovely feature
Nice creature
Sometimes hopper.

Matthew Toplis (11)
Ashleigh Primary School

Our Teacher Kennings

Humourous laughter
Cunning smiler
Hard worker
Good painter
Neat handwriter
Brilliant divider
Excellent researcher
Fantastic drawer
Perfect carer
Champion typer.

Gemma Hulme (10)
Ashleigh Primary School

Haiku - My Snake

My snake is so long
A snake has very strong jaws
It's very greedy.

Charlie Walsh (8)
Ashleigh Primary School

Who?

Cat chaser
Hungry eater
Ball chaser
Loud barker
Funny walker
Fierce biter
Strong fighter
Window scratcher
Great jumper
Food beggar
Human lover
Toy hogger
Strange jogger
Silly dancer
Cat pouncer.

Amy Atherton (10)
Ashleigh Primary School

Who?

Carrot biter
Ear flopper
Bunny bouncer
Angry thumper
Water drinker
High bouncer
Grass eater
Fast runner
Mad bunny
Claw scratcher
Fur licker
Night moaner
Kid biter
Eye blinker.

Natasha Hopwood (11)
Ashleigh Primary School

Cats, Cats, Cats

Wet licker
Leg sitter
Food catcher
Fur scratcher
Night crawler
Plucking harder
Loud purrer
Mouse chaser
Milk slurper
Mad hisser
Tail waggler
Tree banger
Chair sleeper
Tummy rumbler
That's cats.

Tori Brown (10)
Ashleigh Primary School

Hamster Havoc

Food eater
Race cheater
Day sleeper
Food keeper
Cage biter
Chewing lighter
Biting master
Eating faster
Wire chewer
Getting newer
Fur dropper
Bed flopper
Water spiller
Pouch filler.

Joshua Gent (11)
Ashleigh Primary School

Cats

Softly purring
Tails whirring
Hand licker
Fussy picker
Wildly yowling
Midnight howling
Basket sleeper
Night-time creeper
Fast eater
Portable heater
Hand biter
Enemy fighter
Mouse slayer
Happy player
Water hater
Floor skater
Dog resenting
Cats.

Rosie France (10)
Ashleigh Primary School

The Dreaded Dentist!

Teeth puller
Day duller
Gum driller
Tooth filler
Clever feller
Breath smeller
Brace maker
Money taker
Child scarer
Non carer
Big darer!

Miles Starkie (11)
Ashleigh Primary School

My Dog

Tail wagger
Toy snatcher
Water licker
Ball kicker
Meat eater
Mad runner
Basket sleeper
Cat creeper
Long walker
Noisy barker
Fast moulter
Screechy halter
Window breather
Greedy feeder
Loud snorer
Fast waker.

Lauren Berresford (10)
Ashleigh Primary School

Ivy

Ivy
is
like
a
hunting
leopard
it
suffocates
its
prey
with
its
teeth.

Jacob Hesmondhalgh (9)
Ashleigh Primary School

The Jabberwocky

It was brilliant and the slimy toads
Did sing and dance in the shrubs!
All joyous in the towns,
And the citizens were full of bliss.

'Beware of the Jabberwocky my son!'
The jaws that bite, the claws that bite, the claws that catch!
Beware the jub jub bird and avoid
The furious badger eater.

Liam Birkner (11)
Ashleigh Primary School

The Jabberwocky
(Based on 'The Jabberwocky' by Lewis Carroll)

It was brilliant and the slimy toads
Did groan and grunt in the water
All cheerful were the people
And the tiny animals outraged.

He took his deadly sword in hand
Long time the vicious enemy he sought
So rested he by the tall tree
And stood awhile thinking.

Lucy Starkie (11)
Ashleigh Primary School

Isabel, Isabel

Isabel, Isabel met a witch
Isabel, Isabel didn't twitch.
The witch said to Isabel, 'I will turn you into a pie.'
Isabel, Isabel, didn't cry.
Isabel, Isabel, didn't scream or scurry,
Isabel, Isabel, turned the witch into a curry.

Jason Evans (10)
Ashleigh Primary School

The Girl

She stood there in the corridor
While everyone passed by
She never said a single word
Maybe she was shy?

Her hair was greasy and tangled
It looked a great big jumble
But if anyone made fun of her
She didn't give a grumble.

But the girl was always there at school
Even though she wasn't in class
When class was over, everyone pushed her
But she let everyone pass.

One day she wasn't at school oh no!
She wasn't there one day
She wasn't there for a month, then a year
The girl had gone away!

Two years went by and no one saw the girl
Passed by another year
One day I saw the girl, was it my eyes?
I saw her disappear!

I was very scared and frightened
My body was really shaking
I was almost fainting with fright
What a scene I was making!

Never again did I see the girl
The unexpected ghoul
But the day I saw the girl disappear
Was the worst ever day in school!

Maimuna Memon (11)
Ashleigh Primary School

School Nurse

Whenever the school nurse comes,
All the children get the shivers
When she comes into a classroom with her special list
The school bully will shake his fist.
Whenever the school nurse comes,
Whenever the school nurse comes,
She always has a smile on her face,
But that's until we see the black case.
Whatever's in there, nobody knows,
Because when she opens it there's a tingle in our toes.
We close our eyes and faint in horror,
Until she comes again tomorrow.

Lisa Proctor (10)
Ashleigh Primary School

Excuses, Excuses

Why late again, Lakey?
Lost car keys Sir, but got another car Sir.
What happened to the other car?
It was a banger Sir.
Have you got another car Lakey?
Yes Sir.
Where is it?
Ran out of petrol Sir.
What kind of car was it?
Mini Sir.
Mini eh, no wonder that little bug ran out of petrol.

Matthew Lakey (9)
Ashleigh Primary School

Fat Worm

Fat worm's fat
His real name's Mat.
He is so fat and small
He usually gets kicked against the wall.

Fat worm makes great big holes
Sometimes big enough for baby moles.
Fat worm's the fattest of them all
He doesn't get picked for anything at all.

Fat worm's fat, he gets cut in half
But when he does he manages to survive.
He loves green peas
But he hates beans.

Fat worm loves food
But it puts him in a very bad mood.
Fat worm lives in a hole
Thankfully nowhere near his worst friend, the mole.

Joe Bentley (11)
Avondale Primary School

Ladybird

A ladybird lives under a bush
When it rains it's in a rush.
A ladybird tries looking for food
When he's in a bad mood.

Ladybirds fly round and round
He has black circles that are round.
He jumps up high like a clown
And walks around in a dressing gown.

Sam Padbury (11)
Avondale Primary School

Untitled

I caught a snowflake
Falling, falling,
Down from the sky.
I caught a raindrop
And the noise
Went pitter-patter.

Samantha Wright (6)
Avondale Primary School

Untitled

Snowflakes are freezing cold
They freeze your fingers
They freeze your cheeks
Ears and noses go red
Then I go in and get warm.

Jordan Astley (5)
Avondale Primary School

Untitled

The trees are empty and bare
The houses are glittery
And the noses on children are red.
The snowmen have smiley faces.

Alex Worrall (5)
Avondale Primary School

Bonfire - Haiku

Crackling bonfire
Pop, pop, pop, burning, sizzling,
Blazing Guy Fawkes dies.

Carley Gaskell (10)
Avondale Primary School

Ladybird

The ladybird's surroundings are luscious and green
But it's not hard for her to be seen.
With a tiny head and a bright red back,
Different sized spots round and black.

The ladybird's clever and very fast
If you had her in a race you'd definitely be last.
She gets her energy from the greens she eats
And prefers to eat plants rather than meat.

She's kind and funny and likes to make friends
Because she's always there to lend
A helping hand for a friend in need
She'll lend you a game or a book to read.

Ladybird is tidy and very clean
Very friendly and never mean.
She lives on a branch surrounded by leaves
High in the sky, in one of the trees.

Hannah Brown (11)
Avondale Primary School

Warrior Ant

Marching through the stony path
All with weapons and none that laugh
The enemy stomping through the grass,
All standing in a mass.

Now in the burning sands
Through the park through the sandbox in great bands.

The commando ant big and red
All the ants at home hiding in bed.

The enemy strays and strays
The ants approach taking days and days.

Callum Evans (11)
Avondale Primary School

Tigerfly

Creeping up on you from behind,
You can tell right now it isn't very kind.
Tigerfly, tigerfly,
Oh why? Why? Why?

He roars like a tiger,
Except he's much lighter.
Tigerfly, tigerfly,
Oh why? Why? Why?

He doesn't like frogs,
Yet he still visits bogs,
Tigerfly, tigerfly,
Oh why? Why? Why?

When will he get eaten by the dog frog?
When he sits on his little old log.
Tigerfly, tigerfly,
Oh why? Why? Why?

Thurston Thomson (11)
Avondale Primary School

Batdog

Batdog flies above the farm
And when he falls he hurts his arm,
All day long he'll fly around
But when it's night, he'll swoop to the ground.

Batdog walks into town
In his bright pink dressing gown,
He'll go home through the sky
On his own he will fly.

Batdogs chasing a little black cat
Then he hits it with a baseball bat,
He'll walk home through the street,
And go to the shop for a bite to eat.

Bryony Cookson
Avondale Primary School

A Poem About School

The teachers are kind
And there are new friends to find.
The learning is great
That's why I never want to be late.

The dinner is excellent
And I'm never greedy like an elephant.
In school it is fun,
And loads of activities are done.

We are never allowed to take toys
The worst thing is the boys
They're never very good
And they throw each other in mud.

We once found a ball
It was signed by Roald Dahl.
There's people to look after you
And there's always things to do
    In school.

Amy Brogden (8)
Avondale Primary School

White

White is the colour of fluffy white sheep.
White is the colour of crunchy white snow.
White is the colour of a chubby round snowman.
White is the colour of sparkling clean teeth.
White is the colour of bouncing white hailstones.
White is the colour of Santa's cuddly beard.

Alice Brown (7)
Avondale Primary School

Silverbird

Silverbird sleeps on a hill
He loves swooping down to kill
When prey comes and then he hums
Then he eats a lot of buns.

Every day he likes eating
Round and round the field it goes sleeping.
Because it is lazy, now, now, now,
It doesn't know how, how, how.

Riding a bike with his friend
But they ride to the end
Some people think it's rare
Many people say it's a hare.

Silverbird flies in the sky,
Then he eats a great big pie.
Silverbird doesn't like rice,
So he chases little fat mice.

Dean Riding (11)
Avondale Primary School

Spells

Put into the cauldron:

Two silly kittens
Five ugly rats
A bat's tooth
And a squashed banana.

Stir them up with elephant's ear,
And octopus soup.

While you stir
Say this spell . . .

Wobble cobble
Fish jobble
Make a man's tooth grow and grow.

Eve Middlehurst (9)
Avondale Primary School

Flying Elephant

Flying elephant lives in a cloud
Flying elephant is very loud
Flying elephant has magic powers
Flying elephant fights crime for hours.

Flying elephants eats banana splits
But he doesn't like the chocolate bits.
Flying elephant loves to swim
He also very much loves to win.

Flying elephant is very cool
He also very much loves with his friends to play pool.
Flying elephant has a very strict rule,
To keep his house as clean as school.

Flying elephant is very fast
Flying elephant never comes last
Flying elephant glides through the sky
Flying elephant says goodbye.

Charlotte Green (11)
Avondale Primary School

Jaye's Animals

Ten lovely peacocks showing off all day
Nine golden ginger cats scratching the pillows
Eight baby hamsters snoring in a cage
Seven golden fish making bubbles day and night
Six white dogs playing the piano
Five crawling spiders crawling up your legs
Four stripy hissing snakes slithering across the floor
Three fat mice crawling in the pipes
Two hummingbirds humming in the dark
And one
    Guess what?

Jaye Hecker (8)
Avondale Primary School

An Alien Dropped By

It's strange,
An alien dropped by,
It stole some burgers,
I don't know why.

He could think it's a pair of earmuffs,
I think he could have come from Venus?
He has got a big head,
I think he is a genius!

His spaceship was big,
I think he's made of snow,
He had big eyes,
He looked like he could make a pot.

He was funny,
He went like a zip,
He had a smile,
He didn't sign a slip.

Sam Smith (10)
Avondale Primary School

What Is In The Box?

Is it . . .
A spotty ladybird flying?
A hairy caterpillar crawling?
A multicoloured magical unicorn sleeping?
A slippery slug shining?
A slimy worm hissing?
A grey rat running?
A green stickbeetle climbing?
    We don't know
        Let's look.

Jack Thompson (9)
Avondale Primary School

Song Of The Witches

Double, double toil and trouble;
Fire burn and cauldron bubble.
The hand of a clock
And whisker of a cat.
The poison of a snake and
Wing of a bat.
The point of a star and tongue of an ox
The ear of rabbit and nose of a fox.

The bark of a dog
And leg of a hog
The eye of fish
And jar of jam in a dish.

Double, double toil and trouble
Fire burn and cauldron bubble.
Stir it with a earbud,
Then the charm is firm and good.

Stephen Malone (9)
Avondale Primary School

Luke And Jack's Pets

In their bedroom Luke and Jack kept
Ten hamsters snoozing in their cage
Nine rats chasing each other around the room
Eight hairy caterpillars crawling around a jar
Seven fat budgies killing each other
Six black cats sleeping happily
Five big black dogs pawing
Four dirty pigs crying
Three grey donkeys living in a wardrobe
Two rabbits hopping

One guess what?

Luke Atkinson (9)
Avondale Primary School

Song Of The Witches

Double, double toil and trouble,
Fire burn and cauldron bubble.
Wing of bat,
And leg of cat,
Jumping frog,
And walking dog.

A whale's tail
And a wing of a quail
A wolf's howl,
And a brown owl.

Double, double toil and trouble
Fire burn and cauldron bubble.
Stir it up with a plank of wood
Then the charm is firm and good.

Jade Whittaker (9)
Avondale Primary School

Song Of The Witches

Double, double toil and trouble
Fire burn and cauldron bubble
Mix it with a blind man's eye
Black dirty spiders that are sly
Nine eyes of an alien dog
Two big black legs of a frog.

For a bit of weird trouble
It's a bit of a stupid muddle.

Double, double toil and trouble
Fire burn and cauldron bubble
Stir it with a plank of wood
Then the charm is firm and good.

Kayleigh Moir (9)
Avondale Primary School

Haikus

Stormy

Horrible storm strikes
thundering downtown loudly
on a stormy day.

Summer

Warm hot sun shining
melting in the warm sunshine
lovely time to play.

Rain

Rain splitter splatter
on the ground they safely land
falling down the drains.

Sam Elliott (10)
Avondale Primary School

My Pillazard

My Pillazard is furry and round,
The funny thing is it only weighs one pound!
It eats a leaf then has a sleep,
The bed he sleeps on is a big mud heap.

The eyes are stars,
The feet the shape of jam jars.
It smells so strange,
It has no brains.

The way it walks is on two legs,
Its favourite food is boiled eggs.
The feet are yellow, green and blue,
Would you like this pet too?

Rebecca Brandon (10)
Avondale Primary School

Nazia's And Billie's Pets

In their bedroom Nazia and Billie kept
Ten lazy horses snoring
Nine slimy snakes hissing loudly
Eight excited rabbits running around the room
Seven little ladybirds eating green leaves
Six small puppies barking out the window
Five fat rats nibbling in bed
Four small white kittens purring
Three black ants crawling on the blanket
Two goldfish swimming in circles
And one guess what?

Billie Nesfield (9)
Avondale Primary School

What Is In The Box?

Is it
A hungry lion running?
A tiny kangaroo boxing?
A slimy frog jumping?
A little donkey wrestling?
A curly snake sleeping?

    We don't know
    Let's look.

Michael Donnelly (9)
Avondale Primary School

Haiku - Football Match

Rovers have the ball
Cole scored a great goal, one-nil.
They beat Liverpool.

Cara-Beth Grimshaw (9)
Avondale Primary School

Stephen And Jack's Pets

In the bedroom they kept
Ten onions lurking in the toilet
Nine dumb caterpillars barking away
Eight chubby leprechauns drowning in the bath
Seven drunken hamsters sliding in the sink
Six pickled rabbits in a jar
Five smelly rats dangling from the drainpipe
Four books torn
Three black cobras leading out of the basket
Two wires clicking together
And one . . . guess what?

Jack Hutchinson (9)
Avondale Primary School

Blue As . . .

Blue as a reflecting eye
Blue as the pouring rain
Blue as the Earth swirling round
Blue as the shining sky
Blue as sticky Blu-tack
Blue as a tweeting bluebird
Blue as the deep swimming pool
Blue as school literacy books
Blue as a wild bluebell
Blue as a blue handwriting pen.

Grace Charlotte Jepson (8)
Avondale Primary School

Autumn Poetry

Swaying like snowflakes as they fall on the ground
Trees are as big as a giant standing straight and tall.
They make a crunchy carpet on the forest floor.
Leaves as golden as the sun up high in the sky.

Jordan Walmsley (9)
Avondale Primary School

An Alien Stole My Bobble

An alien stole my bobble,
so I let out a scream,
so loud that my mum never
gave me any ice cream.

It was all over
as quick as a flash,
but I'm rather glad
that it didn't last.

But what will they use it for?
Maybe a bracelet?
I really don't know,
maybe for the lace in it?

It could be for a sling shot?
Yes, I'm sure that's why,
to shoot off enemies of aliens,
isn't that us?
Oh my!

Amy Earlam (9)
Avondale Primary School

Haikus

Winter

Icy, white blanket
Children playing in the snow
Spring is coming soon.

Summer

Warm, hot sun shining
The warm sun is in the sky
Autumn is coming.

Tiffany Millsopp (10)
Avondale Primary School

Haikus

Winter

Snow is shimmering
Snowmen standing in the snow
Everything is white.

The Witch

The witch is coming
Ugly pimple on her nose,
Hide or she'll zap you!

A Jungle

It's wet and muddy
Animals creeping around,
Noise is everywhere.

Lucy Morris (9)
Avondale Primary School

Haikus

Winter

Snow comes falling down
Covers houses in the street
All has now turned white.

Tiger

The tiger's roaring
Black and white stripes on his fur
Marching down the lane.

Summer

Sun is coming out
Flowers growing nice and bright
Time to go and play.

Harley Pennington (10)
Avondale Primary School

The Park

Dogs bark on the dry grass,
The ducks quack on the dirty water,
The screams wake the moaning babies,
The babies cry in the prams,
The swings squeak the rusty metal,
The wind howls through the grass,
The girls and boys rustle through the autumn leaves,
The girls' and boys' feet patter on the concrete ground.

Liam Davis (9)
Avondale Primary School

Autumn Poetry

Hedgehogs sleeping under some warm leaves.
As spiky as a conker shell dangling off a branch.
The trees are as big as giants standing straight and tall.
The twisted fingers of branches reach up to the sky.
Leaves as golden as the sun high in the sky.
They sway like snowflakes as they fall to the ground.

Rebekah Cardoo (9)
Avondale Primary School

An Autumn Poem

Leaves are a crunchy carpet on the ground.
Fire is as hot as tea or coffee.
The cold wind is like rocks falling against you.
Mice are balls of fluff scurrying for nuts.
Foxes are as orange as the evening sky.
Squirrels are as soft as a pillow.

Bianca Mizon (10)
Avondale Primary School

The Street

Cats rustling in the bushes.
The howling wind passing through the alleyway.
The dripping of the gutters leaking.
Teenagers chatting about homework.
The sound of laughing because children are having a good time.
The pattering of dogs' paws slapping on the ground.
Doors creaking open and shut.
The crunching of leaves as the wind carries them away.

Rebecca Marsden (9)
Avondale Primary School

The Street

Cats moaning in the alley,
Dogs barking to the neighbours,
Wind howling over the rooftops,
Footsteps pattering past the houses,
Leaves rustling as the wind passes by,
Gutters splashing on the rubbish bins,
Children laughing when friends tell jokes,
Teenagers chattering on the street.

Nicholas Holden (10)
Avondale Primary School

The Park

The ducks quack in the deep river,
Unhappy babies wailing in their prams,
Swings creaking through the air,
Roundabouts swirling round and round,
Dogs barking through the day,
Children swooshing down the slide,
Old leaves crunching on the ground,
The wind howling through the trees.

Jack Sims (10)
Avondale Primary School

Haikus

Football Match

Beckham scores a goal
Owen runs right up the pitch
One-nil to England.

Witch

The cat is a pain
So is the evil woman
But we can't help that.

Bradley Harper (10)
Avondale Primary School

Haikus

Chips

Chips hot and salty
They're better wrapped in paper
Juicy, nice and fat.

Summer

Warm, hot sun shining,
Ice cream melting in my hand
Lying on the sand.

Jordan Taylor
Avondale Primary School

Hallowe'en

Black cat staring evilly,
Sooty cauldron bubbling noisily,
Rotten nails curling dangerously,
Beastly broomstick floating meanly,
Vile witch cackling nastily.

Emma Marsden (9)
Avondale Primary School

Haikus

A Tiger

Here comes a huge cat,
Roaring as it comes my way,
An orange tiger.

Food

Twelve o'clock has come,
Children rushing to the hall,
Food is being served.

Winter

A big white snowman
Snow is falling in the air,
The weather is cold.

Emma Dudley (9)
Avondale Primary School

The Party Day

The children are laughing excitedly
The music is blaring out deafeningly
Voices yelling out loud
Happy hands are clapping merrily
The mouths are munching busily
Sound of slurping fills the air.

Charlotte Grainger (9)
Avondale Primary School

Haiku - A Football Match

Kick-off at Villa,
With Roar the mascot there too
Fans cheer Rovers on.

Katherine Byrne (10)
Avondale Primary School

Happiness And Sadness

Happiness is if my cat comes back.
Sadness is when I lost my cat.
Happiness is when I went to Manjiamos for my birthday.
Sadness is when I cut my knee open by falling off my
                               bike into plastic chairs.
Happiness is when I am snuggled in my bed.
Sadness is losing your best friend.
Happiness is learning something new.
Happiness and sadness are . . .

Nikki Henry
Avondale Primary School

The Street

Cats moaning in the alleyway,
Dogs barking to the neighbours,
Wind howling over the rooftops,
Footsteps pattering past the houses,
Leaves rustling as the wind passes by,
Gutters splashing on the rubbish bins,
Children laughing when friends tell jokes,
Teenagers chattering on the street.

Jordan Kinsley-Smith (10)
Avondale Primary School

Tigers - Haiku

Tigers

Tigers search for lunch,
Now creeping in the darkness,
Quickly climbs up trees.

Adam Lang (9)
Avondale Primary School

An Alien Stole My Fish!

This is strange,
But it is true,
A really small alien,
Popped out of my loo.

It hopped around the house,
In a bit of a hurry,
I tried to be brave,
But I did start to worry.

It picked up my fish
Then hopped out the door
But I stayed inside,
I didn't see more.

Yes, I do know what he looked like,
He had such a big bum,
Then I remembered,
He looked like my mum.

Georgia Lennon (9)
Avondale Primary School

Happiness

Happiness is in winter when me and my friends
have snowball fights,
Happiness is when me and my dog go for
walks in the woods,
Happiness is seeing dogs every day,
Happiness is getting money and presents,
Happiness is getting celebration chocolate,
Happiness is playing pool,
Happiness is my family and pets.
Happiness is . . .

Kyle Craven (9)
Avondale Primary School

Aliens Stole My Cat

The aliens stole my cat
They might think it's a donkey
or something like that.
It's true, I'm not lying, you have to believe me.

They might put it in a cage and then in a museum
or they could use it as a target for a bow and arrow
or maybe if they put wings on
it could be a sparrow.

They might think she's good and worship her
or that she's bad,
if they did they would probably chuck her out
or they might think she's a lad.

But if she doesn't move or anything like that
they might think she's dead
or just ill,
they might put her to bed.

Zoe Charnock (10)
Avondale Primary School

Happiness

Happiness is having creamy and chocolate
ice cream and chocolate cake,
Sadness is when my sister fights and
screams at me,
Happiness is snuggling in my bed
when it's raining,
Sadness is when I can't go to town in the
misty chilly weather,
Happiness is when me, my sister and my mum
go to Blackpool in the hot air,
Sadness is when I lose my favourite cosy teddy bear.
Happiness is . . .

Zahira Mitha (9)
Avondale Primary School

Song Of The Witches

Double, double toil and trouble
Fire burn and cauldron bubble.
A bit of flannel,
And an ear of a camel,
Put stars in,
And Mars in a bin.

A fox's tail,
And eye of a whale.
A tooth of shark,
And a bit of tree bark.

Double, double toil and trouble
Fire burn and cauldron bubble.
Stir it up with a plank of wood
Now the charm is firm and good.

Jade Eaton (9)
Avondale Primary School

My Dolphincrock

My dolphincrock is very pleasant,
even though he acts like a pheasant,
he snaps and snaps,
and has a good nap.

He eats like a pig,
and wears a very nice wig.
I wonder why,
he has big eyes.

He has a big snout
and likes to pout,
he has gorgeous eyes,
he likes to toll lies!

Charlotte Tattersall (11)
Avondale Primary School

School - Haikus

The bell starts ringing,
Oh no! Now it's time for school,
Hope home time comes soon.

It is dinner time,
I am having chips and beans,
Then I'm playing out.

I am going home,
Because school has just finished,
Tomorrow's Friday.

Jack Mills (9)
Avondale Primary School

Hallowe'en

Nasty witch cackling evily,
Bubbling cauldron stirring dangerously,
Mean eyes staring sneakily,
Starless moon hanging menacingly,
Black cloak curling meanly,
Beastly broomsticks whizzing wickedly.

Sophie Bannister (9)
Avondale Primary School

The Witch

Wicked witch flying evily
Nasty cat staring horribly
Black hat sitting spookily
Sharp nose pointing meanly
Big castle standing darkly.

Andrea Cooney (9)
Avondale Primary School

Happiness

Happiness is having a little cute Labrador,
Happiness is going to South Africa and seeing my other friends,
Happiness is going to the swimming baths and going on the slide,
Happiness is getting new Pokemon cards and trading
them with my friends,
Happiness is staying up late and watching movies
and eating snacks,
Happiness is getting a quad bike and riding around fast,
Happiness is getting presents at Christmas
and seeing what there is,
Happiness is . . .

Michael Clarke (9)
Avondale Primary School

Sadness And Happiness

Happiness is when my dog jumps on me and licks me,
Sadness is when I lose all my friends in class,
Happiness is when I have all my snuggly teddies,
Sadness is when I don't have a dog to play with,
Happiness is when I get lots of chocolates at Christmas,
Sadness is when I am grounded in my bedroom,
Sadness and happiness are . . .

Chloe Brierley (9)
Avondale Primary School

Autumn

Soft rain falls like angels' teardrops.
Foxes are cheetahs running through the fields.
Night is a dark thief stealing the daylight.
Squirrels are as soft as a pillow.
Mice are soft balls of fluff.
Hedgehogs are as prickly as a cactus.

Amy Towers (9)
Avondale Primary School

Swordfish

He lives deep in the depths of the ocean,
And attacks those without motion,
He eats fish smaller than himself,
And when he's hurt he always regains health.

Attached to his face is a razor-sharp blade,
But down in the ocean he is lightly weighed.
He lives in a cave on the seabed,
Any who enter are overcome with dread.

It plots slyly in its hiding place,
And pounces on those with a slow pace.
His cunning, darting eyes fixed on his prey,
Any moment there will be one less fish in the sea today.

This creature has a daring mind,
Like all the others of its kind,
Pacing the seabed to and fro,
Swordfish, a deadly foe.

Faye Hutchinson (11)
Avondale Primary School

Autumn

Autumn leaves are falling down,
Orange, red, yellow and brown,
See them swirling in the wind,
And floating to the ground.

Autumn leaves are swirling round,
Laying a crunching carpet down,
The world fills with colours like a crown,
Till winter comes and snow falls down.

Christopher Entwisle (11)
Avondale Primary School

Racehorse

Racehorse running fast
Racehorse never last
Racehorse dashing by
Racehorse jumping high.

Racehorse like a flash
Racehorse there's a crash.
Racehorse gold and brown
Racehorse messing around.

Racehorse coming past
Racehorse chasing fast
Racehorse off course
Racehorse my horse.

Racehorse never slow
Racehorse 1st place bow
Racehorse you're the best
Racehorse have a rest.

Kristan-Leigh Jennison (10)
Avondale Primary School

Dogstick

My dogstick is my favourite pet
He moves in a funky way
I hope he won't leave me yet,
But he will do some day.

Dogstick is a funny net,
He always tries his best,
But if he is in a funny mood,
He gets stuck in a net!

Jessica Lewis (10)
Avondale Primary School

Animal Alphabet

You go to a zoo
To look at the animals
But they're all looking at you,

Ants crawl to you
Badgers run to you
Camels spit at you
Dolphins moan at you
Eagles fly towards you
Falcons shout at you
Goats chase you
Hippopotamus chomp at you
Insects look at you
Jellyfish sting you
Kittens miaow at you
Lions roar at you
Monkey laugh at you
Newts swim to you
Octopus squirt ink at you
Pigs snarl at you
Quails cheep at you
Rabbits jump at you
Spiders climb up you
Tarantulas face you
Unicorns stare at you
Vulcans stand on you
Whales squirt water at you
Yaks glare at you
Zebras trot to you.

You go to a zoo
To look at the animals
But they're all looking at you!

Ryan Swanepoel (8)
Avondale Primary School

An Alien Stole My Sock

An alien came into my bedroom
and walked right over to my drawer,
It took out a sock, left a slime trail
I hope it doesn't leave any more.

It got hold of my cover
He looked like my mum.
I started to get scared,
Because he had a big bum!

It fell out of bed
Then it had a sore head,
He jumped out the window,
It looked like he was dead.

The alien went back in his saucer,
And had a big roar.
Something opened
It was the door.

I looked out the window
And saw the alien with my sock in its hand,
So I made a sign that said
Aliens are banned!

Devon-Louise McKenna (9)
Avondale Primary School

The Beach - Haiku

The beach

Children having fun
Adults sunbathing all day
Big waves crashing down.

Matthew McKeown (9)
Avondale Primary School

Haikus

Chips

Chips, hot and salty
wrapped up in some newspaper
juicy, nice and hot.

Summer

The warm hot sun shines
eating freezing cold ice cream
lying in the sand.

Rain

Rain, spitter, splatter
Down comes the rain, splish, splash, splosh,
splash in the puddles.

Adam Loonat (10)
Avondale Primary School

Cowshee (Cow/Sheep)

My Cowshee has a candyfloss coat,
Big brown eyes,
And a leathery throat.

My Cowshee has huge grey hooves,
Short black legs,
And look how she moves.

My Cowshee has a long fluffy tail,
A big wet nose,
And a screeching wail.

My Cowshee has large plodding strides
A sluggish sprint,
And she really loves rides.

Charlotte Rosson (11)
Avondale Primary School

Racehorse

Racehorse running around
dashing all about.
Racehorse running around
you want to hear him shout.
Racehorse he never stops
you always see him fly right by.
Racehorse running by
he runs as fast as a baby's cry.

Racehorse never last
Racehorse cannot fly
Racehorse galloping past
Racehorse running by.

Racehorse stop being lazy
Racehorse stop being crazy
Racehorse dark brown
Racehorse stop messing around.

Anthony Ellis (11)
Avondale Primary School

Rabyin

He jumps without springs.
He eats all my things.
Low in my garden,
He squeaks and sings.

He ate the teacher's chalk
He attacked the old folk
Running down the street,
He got caught by my friend Pete.

My rabyin is my favourite pet,
A better pet you've never met.
He's so sweet said my friend Pete,
But my dog he doesn't beat.

Lee Marsden (11)
Avondale Primary School

Grumpy Worm

Grumpy worm lives in the ground,
He really hates slithering around,
Grumpy worm is very lazy,
Sometimes he gets hyperactive and is very crazy.

Grumpy worm eats in the sun,
Grumpy worm has lots of fun,
Grumpy worm loves to swim,
Grumpy worm loves to sing a hymn.

Grumpy worm loves to play,
But only when it's a nice day,
Grumpy worm loves to eat,
But doesn't like pig meat.

Grumpy worm falls asleep,
But sometimes he oversleeps,
Grumpy worm loves to dance,
But would prefer to go to France.

Stephanie Cooke
Avondale Primary School

The Street

Cats rustling in the bushes
The howling wind passing through the alleyway
The dripping of the gutters leaking,
Teenagers chatting about homework
The sound of laughing because they're having a good time
The pattering of a dog's paws slapping on the ground
Doors creaking as they open and shut
The crunching of leaves as the wind carries them away.

Rebecca Bromley (9)
Avondale Primary School

Monrat

Monrat's tail is thin and hairy,
and his eyes are very blary.
Monrat has very big eyes,
he has bulging lips for eating flies.

Monrat has a very thin nose,
any time he will have a nap or a doze.
It has very big hairy hands,
and is extremely good at making plans.

Monrat is very lazy
and when he runs around he acts crazy.
Monrat's ears are like gel,
the owner of Monrat is called Mell.

He is a real pain,
stronger than a Great Dane!
Monrat sleeps in the shed at night,
we don't like him because he gives our neighbours
a big fright.

David Helmn (10)
Avondale Primary School

Autumn Poetry

As spiky as a conker shell dangling from a tree,
Hedgehogs sleep under warm leaves.

The trees are as big as giants standing straight and tall,
The thin twisted fingers of branches reach up in the sky.

Berries are as red as blood dripping down my leg,
Lying on the ground as shiny as jewels.

Leaves swaying like snowflakes as they flutter to the ground,
As golden as the sun shining in the sky.

Sophie Ashcroft (9)
Avondale Primary School

It's The 5th November - Haiku

Guy Fawkes burning bright
Exploding fireworks shine
As the embers die.

Josie Bury (10)
Avondale Primary School

The Spider - A Haiku

In the dark corners
Of the deep cave, something creeps
Gently, soft, silent.

Eight legs on silk web
Perfectly spun and graceful
Its whole life support.

Unsuspecting prey
Caught in the mass of tangles
Waiting for its death.

Alex Watson (10)
Brinscall St John's CE Primary School

An Autumn Poem

The skeletal tree is an overhanging skyscraper,
being shelled heavily by the dim sunlight.

The colossal grey sky, in which the smoky clouds lie,
Is a thick barrier surrounding the tense battlefield of
dew-covered grass.

The brown crisp leaves are killer bullets,
launched off the trees by the raging wind
that screams the siren of war.

Matthew Parsons (10)
Brinscall St John's CE Primary School

Heaven Is . . .

A world with fluffy, bright clouds,
A welcoming place where you meet up with
all your long-lost relatives,
A sparkling gold gate leading to a place
where people no longer suffer,
A fairy-tale castle where angels live and
bring glory to the heavens,
An island where Jesus lets only the good
people on Earth enter.

Georgina Hackett (9)
Brinscall St John's CE Primary School

Heaven Is . . .

A world of delicious treats waiting to be eaten,
A giant hand shielding you from all your fears,
A golden chariot whisking you away to a
                           wondrous dreamland,
A fluffy cloud lit by sweet silver candles,
An ocean of gleaming diamonds coated in soft bronze.

Nicole van der Linde (10)
Brinscall St John's CE Primary School

Heaven Is . . .

A golden light shining through white fluffy clouds.
A harp played by a heavenly angel.
A gold gate standing on the clouds.
Trumpets blasting out for the return of a white
snowy barn owl with a dove.

Katie Rigby (9)
Brinscall St John's CE Primary School

War, An Autumn Poem

The sun is trapped in a net of dark mist,
it fights for survival, a soldier in a war.

The cruel frost is free to roam once again,
it takes over everything in sight,
it freezes the bloody war field.

The wind fights the frost, and wins,
it blows and howls its mighty call.

The trees fight the wind and succeed in winning,
they spread the seed of life once again.

Grace Davies (10)
Brinscall St John's CE Primary School

Heaven Is . . .

The gate to life.
Its huge, diamanté engraved silver gates open,
To show you the light at the end of the tunnel.
The long strip of cloud is full of newcomers.
The hotel room where you live, suited to fit your standards.
When you die your conscience forms an extra body
And becomes the voice.
The life of Heaven is just like the rich and famous.

Kay Shuttleworth (10)
Brinscall St John's CE Primary School

Heaven Is . . .

A cushiony palace surrounded by sparkly tints of gold.
A fragranced paradise with a fluorescent smell of
                                      apple blossom.
A block of peace circles its unique, skeletal walls,
Guarding its hidden treasures.
Heaven is pure.

Isaac Worthington (10)
Brinscall St John's CE Primary School

A Night In Africa

As people come together,
And sit down under the bright moon,
The stars crowd over,
Watching with amazement,
Fruit bats soar above their heads,
Puzzled with the excitement of laughter.

Hands beating on fur drums,
Feet tapping on the sandy floor,
The flames dance upon the burning logs,
An orange glow from the fire,
Spreads the warmth onto happy faces,
African children smiling and laughing,
A night in Africa!

Ceri Yates (11)
Brinscall St John's CE Primary School

Perfect Picture

Sky, blue exuberant colours,
Merry red, joyful green, inside my head.
Peace, perfect brightness,
Dancing daisies, skipping through the jewelled golden meadows.
Miles of brilliant fields, free to go your way.
No cities, no towns, no pollution . . .
Just open ground . . .
The country world spreads throughout the land,
Nothing knowing anything of human existence
or beyond that world.

Oliver Horrocks (9)
Brinscall St John's CE Primary School

This Is Wildlife

Lion is a fuming, roaring fire,
Lurking upon his cautious prey,
Colossal elephant is cunning
And wise, stomping through the grassy plains.
Wildlife - the wonderful
Wildlife!

Zebras huddle together
In a herd, ears twitching,
Alert,
Hasty, male leopards compel
Their army of cubs to hunt
And fend for themselves.
Wildlife - the wonderful
Wildlife!

Hannah Kirkman (11)
Brinscall St John's CE Primary School

Who Am I?

I am the one who annoys the hot people,
I am the one who gets deckchairs out,
I am the one who sneaks into houses,
Who do you think I am?

I am the one who pleases the animals,
I am the one who gives them a warm bed,
I am the one who makes them tired,
Who do you think I am?

I am the one who affects Africa,
I am the one who gives it its strong warmth,
I am the one who keeps the harsh cold away,
I am the wonderful heat.

Tobi Brown (11)
Brinscall St John's CE Primary School

Africa

Sand gathered round the ground,
One tree in the distance,
Is it a mirage?
This is Africa.

Animals, enormous and compact,
Feasting on different textures everywhere,
Poachers surround them, startle the animals,
This is Africa.

Beautiful orange sun gliding down below the Earth,
Pink clouds hovering over the dark land below.
Red, pink and black, covered our country,
This is Africa.

Plains of fresh grass rustle,
Tree leaves rustle to the floor,
Nothing in sight except green, green, green.
This is Africa.

Cities and towns destroy Africa,
Traditions fade away far away,
Look what we have done to our country,
This is Africa.

Madelyn Smith (10)
Brinscall St John's CE Primary School

An African Desert

The desert swirls and dances,
as the air brushes through the sand like a comb.

The awesome warmth soars through the air,
before settling on the soft, golden sand underfoot.

As the day blends into night,
Dust swivels around the sun, hiding it throughout the night.

An African desert is a magical place.

Freya Metters (10)
Brinscall St John's CE Primary School

A Jungle To Explore

A jungle to explore, lots of things to see,
Or it might just seem like that to you and me.

But people have to live in the vast wasteland,
Non variety of food to eat,
No good water to drink,
Starving children because there's not enough food
to go around
So is it really that great?

A jungle to explore, lots of things to see
Or it might just seem like that to you and me.

It may not seem like it to you and me,
but cities are aplenty
Kifo, just one of them
School, shops and TV, brick houses, cars, pubs,
So isn't life just the same?

A jungle to explore, lots of things to see,
Maybe it just seems like that to you and me.

Harry Mullett (10)
Brinscall St John's CE Primary School

Desert

The gritty sand dances across the uninhabited desert,
baking the wasteland below.

The fiery sun grins at his work,
as sand dunes topple to their death.

The wilderness proceeds towards surrounding villages,
burying cultures in her centre.

The desert's getting larger all the time,
Could you survive its temper?

Helen Savage (11)
Brinscall St John's CE Primary School

The Course Of An African River

I look upon an African river
My eyes fill with beauty beyond my wildest dreams,
The crystal clear water reflects the brilliant blue sky
And the blazing sun giving it a glitter that could even stun the leopard.

The river comes to an elephant, it weaves in and out
                              of its ginormous legs,
Picking away at the flecks of dirt on its ginormous feet.
The monkey swings from tree to tree following the rushing
river's progress until it comes to the edge of a drop.

The river will jump off the edge of the drop,
Rushing down faster than a bird transforming itself into
                                a waterfall,
It hits the bottom and turns into white foam,
Stirring the silent river and making a sound that trembles
                                the ear drums.

But the river has a greater purpose than cleaning the elephant,
It provides water for the people who live in little mud huts,
Nobody really appreciates what the dashing river does.

Emily Burgoyne (10)
Brinscall St John's CE Primary School

Born With Pride

The grasslands are vast empty spaces in the
                              scorching sun,
The sand dunes are mountains towering over Africa,
The jungle is an animal city crawling with animals.

The warriors are lions prowling over the plains searching
                                  for prey,
The people are snakes slipping along through mud huts,
The tribes are camels trokking high into the sunsets

Africa is like an animal born with pride!

Grace Frost (10)
Brinscall St John's CE Primary School

Far Across The Desert Sands

Sand, like an ongoing plain,
Screeching deep out into the horizon,
A gateway impossible to breach,
Like a maze without an end.

But past the sands are distant lands,
Glimmering in the summer sun,
Crystal pools, shady trees,
Shimmering in the breeze.

Herds of elephants,
Monkeys scrambling up trees,
Tribes pillaging helpless villages,
Burning them to the ground.

Far across the desert sands,
Peering into distant lands,
Elephants, monkeys, charging tribes,
Filling you with feel good vibes.

Robert Knowles (11)
Brinscall St John's CE Primary School

Indian Dance

Drums beating,
Pipes screeching,
Awful,
Shaky,
Squeaky,
High-pitched voices,
Strange.

Arms rolling,
Heads nodding,
Shaky,
Fast,
Spinning,
Circular ring dance,
Strange.

Neil Parkinson (9)
Brinscall St John's CE Primary School

Happy Festival

Happy festival,
All dancing,
Moving lips,
Moving legs,
Swinging hips,
Tingling fingers,
Bright colours,
Red, orange, blue,
All cheering,
Song from a bird,
Whooping,
Dance starting slowly,
Getting quicker,
Laughter and clapping
Pipes screeching
Drums beating
Happy festival.

Bethany Briggs (8)
Brinscall St John's CE Primary School

Indian Dance

Pipes are piping,
Drums are drumming,
I wonder what it is?
People dancing,
Shouting, praising,
I wonder what it is?
Ring of dancers,
Bright colours,
I wonder what it is?
The smell of blazing fire,
Strange cooking smells,
I wonder what it is?

Frederick Frost (9)
Brinscall St John's CE Primary School

Indian Song

Strange sounds from a far off place,
High pitched voices,
Faces smiling, happy and jolly,
Beating drums, clapping hands,
People dancing and arms rolling.
Sounds get louder, the voices get higher,
Colours bright yellow and orange,
Fast movements, waving and twirling.

Elle Rossall (9)
Brinscall St John's CE Primary School

Indian Dance

They play lots of instruments
Especially the drums
They jump up and down whilst
Playing the pipes
They jump up and down whilst
Singing their songs
They are telling a story whilst
Dancing around.

Christopher Kirkman (9)
Brinscall St John's CE Primary School

Africa

The trees are monstrous
as they stretch up into the sky.
Watching the leopard ripping its
prey apart.

Even the sand tries to hide
from the scorching hot beams
that blaze down on the dry empty desert.

Josh Almond (11)
Brinscall St John's CE Primary School

Indian Festival

Today is the festival
The jolly happy one
Feet tapping
Hands clapping
People having fun
Around a circle
Around the pole
Starting quiet, getting louder
Fast dancing, bright colours
Glittering in the sunlight.

Nicola Green (8)
Brinscall St John's CE Primary School

Indian Dancers

Indians starting to dance
Pipes were blowing
Hands were clapping
Swaying from side to side
Jumping through the wind
Drums echoing in the air
Shrieking
Shouts
Screams.

Alice Hume (9)
Brinscall St John's CE Primary School

Eagle

Gliding through the air,
Diving up and down,
Flying rapidly looking for meat,
Scooping down to catch prey,
Then up to eat what he has caught.

Charlotte Savage (9)
Brinscall St John's CE Primary School

Indian Dances

Feet tapping
Drums beating
Hands clapping
What could it be?
It's a festival,
Families waving,
Children cheering,
Grandads dancing,
It's a festival!

Oliver Yates (9)
Brinscall St John's CE Primary School

Indian Festival

Happy, dancing people,
Swaying their hips,
Side to side like birds,
Flying in the sky,
People talking,
Yelling a happy story
To everyone,
An amazing beat.

Lewis Richardson (8)
Brinscall St John's CE Primary School

Indian Dance

I can hear birds whooping
People dancing to the beat
I can see moving hips
How on earth can they stand this heat?
It sounds like they're having a festival,
Wearing blue, yellow and red.
All the people are dancing,
And shaking their heads.

Emily Yates (9)
Brinscall St John's CE Primary School

Indian Dance

The colours of this joyful dance
Are bright yellow, red and blue.
The movements of this happy dance
Are swaying and shaking.
The sound of this amusing dance,
Is strange drum beats with shouts and screams,
The instruments of this loud dance
Are pipes, voices and drums.

Richard Ryding (9)
Brinscall St John's CE Primary School

Indian Festival

There's a bird in a tree
Who's singing, laughing,
Having a joyful time,
Watching the clapping,
Feet moving side to side,
People having a good time,
Hands are tapping on their knees,
Fingers are clicking to the beat.

Jessica Taylor (8)
Brinscall St John's CE Primary School

Indian Dance

I hear the sound of joy
I hear the sound of happiness
I see bright colours shining
I see people dancing to the beat
I hear pipes sounding
I hear drums banging
I see people telling a story
I see heads moving from side to side.

Rachael Wheeler (9)
Brinscall St John's CE Primary School

I Know A Pencil

I know a pencil,
Full of lead,
It dances around my window ledge.
It reads my mind,
It smells so fine,
It has lots of money,
It's so funny,
It smells like honey,
Ha ha honey!

Sally Booth (7)
Brinscall St John's CE Primary School

Dancing Song

The beating of drums,
The rhythm of pipes,
Twirling, swirling,
Dancing way into the night.
Fingers are tapping,
Hands are clapping,
People dancing,
Dancing way into the night.

Alice Powell (8)
Brinscall St John's CE Primary School

Indian Party

Dancing and shrieking,
In the orange grass,
Swaying and twirling,
Shaking of maracas,
Blowing of pipes,
High-pitched voices,
Singing with the light.

Matthew Winterson (8)
Brinscall St John's CE Primary School

The Panda

Pandas are fluffy and cuddly.
They live in grass.
Their colour is black and white.
They are huge and have fluffy feet
And have fluffy arms,
As well as a fluffy tummy.
They are lovely and beautiful,
It is a beautiful bear,
It is a fluffy white and black lovely bear.

Jacob Rose (7)
Brinscall St John's CE Primary School

Snow

I like the snow
It's better than a bow.
So ho ho.
Snow is soft
Snow is best but I'll have a rest.
Snow is good, it's better than a hood.
Snow is best but it's not better than a chest.
So don't be a pest.
Snow is the best weather that's better than all the rest.

Jake Whitworth (7)
Brinscall St John's CE Primary School

Rainy Days

Rainy days are always bad,
I'm stuck inside which makes me sad,
At least I can play some games,
Like 'Guess Who', where you've got to find their names.

Olivia Day (7)
Brinscall St John's CE Primary School

Indian Festival

The festival started with cheering
When the drums got louder and louder,
They dance so fast, so very twizzy,
And start tapping in a circle.

The hands started clapping,
When questions were being answered,
The pink pipes got blown so quickly,
They arched around, screaming.

Then the festival ended with a story,
With wonders filling your head,
Ends with a happy ending,
Prayers for their lives desires.

Georgina Ruffin (8)
Brinscall St John's CE Primary School

Indian Dance

Happy,
Jolly,
It makes me feel pink.
Up and down sounds.
Dancers jiggling,
Happy,
Jolly,
Dancers jotting in circles,
Round and round,
Up and down,
People waiting for night.

Katie Ainscough (9)
Brinscall St John's CE Primary School

Middle Ages Battlefield

In battle you just should fight,
Until your enemies are out of sight.
Mount your crossbows,
Nurse your hurt foes.
Fight hand to hand combat,
Kill that French brat.
Block with your shield,
Fight with the sword that you wield.

In a tournament you just should joust,
You use a lance like a mast.
Charge at another man,
You have beside you a nice fan.
Hit the man which is the other,
Do not hit the horse or you'll be in
Trouble with your mother.

Edward Dearden (7)
Brinscall St John's CE Primary School

My Shadow

I saw my shadow on the wall,
I was small but he was tall.
I tried to jump all night, to step on the wall,
But I was too tall.
I tried to jump on it but I couldn't.

I got my shadow out to play,
It played tig with me all day.
It tagged me before I got it,
I see my shadow everyday.

I can see my shadow all the time,
I know he's there all the time.
He listens to what I've said.

Alicia Howarth (7)
Brinscall St John's CE Primary School

Rain, Rain

I hear the rain,
I hear somebody in deep pain,
I hear the rain,
Flooding the drain.
I hear the rain,
Splatting on the lane.
I hear the rain,
Splashing on Jane.
I hear the rain,
Hitting a cane.
I hear the rain,
Hitting a window frame.
I hear the rain, hit a chain.
I hear the rain,
Hitting a train.
I hear the rain,
Again, again, again.

Christopher Parkinson (7)
Brinscall St John's CE Primary School

Fly Away

When you're feeling dumb,
Don't let yourself feel dumb,
Just fly away with me,
And your worries will be history.
I really think you should come,
Then you won't feel dumb.

When you're feeling bad,
Don't go crying to your dad.
Just fly away with me,
And your worries will be history.
I really think you should come,
Then you won't feel bad.

Matthew van der Linde (8)
Brinscall St John's CE Primary School

The Sun

The sun is hot,
And extremely bright.
It is what
Forms day and night.

It's made from gas
And maybe fire.
I think it has
A big desire.

It is so big,
Much bigger than Earth.
Outside it is
Planet Earth.

It's not so tiny,
Although it's a star.
It sits away,
Really far.

Bradley Hardy (8)
Brinscall St John's CE Primary School

Colours

I see red
I see white
I see black
I see blue
I see green
I see grey
I see purple
I see orange
I see brown
I see pink
I see yellow
I see a rainbow
I see a pot of gold.

Jac Vincent (8)
Brinscall St John's CE Primary School

Indian Music

Jingling bells, beating drums,
People singing,
The beat goes on with joy,
Jolly,
Happy,
Telling, dreaming about good things,
People swishing, tapping too the beat,
Sliding, swirling up and down,
Dancing around a pot,
Rice smelling sweet,
Orange, red and brightly coloured music.

Rachel Stringfellow (8)
Brinscall St John's CE Primary School

The Adventures Of Jonathan

Jonathan met a mysterious shark,
Jonathan, Jonathan, got some bark.
The shark was big, the shark was fat,
And the shark swims like a rat.
The shark was long, the shark had a tongue,
And it went pong.
Jonathan, Jonathan, didn't run away,
Jonathan, Jonathan, wanted to stay.
He washed his hands and had a cough,
Then Jonathan chopped the shark's head off.

Jonathan met an enormous snake
Jonathan, Jonathan, saw a lake.
The snake was long, the snake was fat
And the snake's big teeth were as big as a bat.
The snake was strong, the snake sang a song,
Jonathan did something wrong,
Jonathan, Jonathan did not run away,
Jonathan, Jonathan wanted to stay,
He saw the lake
And drowned the snake.

Martyn McLean (9)
Burscough Village Primary School

The Adventures Of Jonathan

Jonathan met a dragon in a huge cave
The dragon looked big and brave
The dragon was hungry, the dragon was ravenous
The dragon's big mouth was cruel and cavernous.
The dragon said,'Jonathan glad to meet you,
How do Jonathan, now I'll eat you!'
Jonathan, Jonathan didn't worry,
Jonathan didn't scream or scurry
He put his hair up and washed his hands,
Then Jonathan ate the dragon up.

Jonathan met a snake
He thought it was a rake.
It had a swim in the lake
And it had a date.
The snake said, 'Jonathan, glad to meet you,
How do Jonathan, I'll kill you!'
Jonathan, Jonathan didn't worry
Jonathan didn't scream or scurry,
Jonathan put on his cape,
And the snake tried to escape.

Jonathan met a hideous giant
Jonathan continued to be self-reliant.
The giant was scary, the giant was horrid,
He had eyes in the middle of his head.
'Good morning Jonathan,' the giant said.
'I'll eat your bones for my bread.'
Jonathan, Jonathan didn't worry
Jonathan didn't scream or scurry.

Jonathan McDonald (10)
Burscough Village Primary School

The Mysteries Of Margaret

Margaret met a hideous lizard,
Margaret, Margaret, bumped into a wizard.
The lizard was scary, the lizard was taily,
The lizard met a friend called Hayley.
The lizard said,'Oh, ho, hello Margaret, glad to meet you,
Now Margaret I will eat you!'
Margaret, Margaret, wasn't in a hurry,
Margaret didn't think to scurry.
She jumped on a chair,
Then Margaret pulled out one of his hairs.

Margaret met an enormous elephant,
Margaret, Margaret wasn't that intelligent.
The elephant balanced his foot over her head,
But before he stood on her, she went to bed.
She woke up and his foot was still there,
She pricked his foot and Margaret didn't run with a scare.
Margaret, Margaret, wasn't in a hurry,
Margaret didn't think to scurry.
She turned on the fan,
And hit him on the head with a frying pan.

Kerris Halsall (10)
Burscough Village Primary School

Christopher's Adventure

Christopher met a robot mum,
Christopher, Christopher thought he'd have fun.
The mum was scary, the mum was strict,
The mum was a person whom he had tricked.
The mum said, 'Christopher, glad to meet you,
Now my son I will beat you.'
Christopher, Christopher didn't worry,
Christopher didn't shout or hurry.
He sharpened a needle and poked her in the eye,
Then said quietly, 'Now you can die.'

Christopher met a crocodile,
A type that swam the River Nile.
The croc was long, the croc was thin,
The croc was almost very dim.
The croc said, 'Christopher, I hope you're happy,
Because I can get very snappy.'
Christopher, Christopher, didn't worry,
Christopher didn't shout or hurry.
He grabbed a stick and put it in his jaws
Then got some pliers and cut off his claws.

Christopher May (9)
Burscough Village Primary School

The Unusual Adventures Of Daniel And His Dog

Danny and his family got a pet,
It ate everything, even the vet!
A person said, 'It eats everything,
Except strawberry chewy string.'
Danny and his friend were playing at night,
The dog came out and started to fight.
Danny got the big thick chain,
Put it around the dog's neck again.
He took it to the doctor,
The doctor cured it with his woolly jumper.

Danny and his dog met a kung fu champ
The kung fu champ said his name was Frank.
The kung fu champ said, 'Do you want to fight?'
Danny said, 'Alright.'
Danny's dog saw a chocolate bar,
But it was a bad remote control car.
Danny got the big thick chain,
Put it round the dog's neck again,
Danny poked the kung fu champ in the eye,
And then he went home to cry.

Danny and his dog met a snake,
His dog thought it was a rake.
The snake was fat, the snake was big,
The snake's mouth was like a pig's.
Danny's dog was about to eat it,
But instead he just bit it.
Danny got the big thick chain,
Put it around the dog's neck again.
Danny said, 'Go away.'
The snake said, 'OK.'

Daniel Caunce (9)
Burscough Village Primary School

The Adventures Of Amanda

Amanda met a robot teacher
Amanda, Amanda, knew he was a preacher.
The teacher was round, the teacher was fat,
The teacher was thick, but he looked like a rat.
The teacher said, 'Amanda glad to meet you,
Now my darling I will teach you!'
Amanda, Amanda didn't cry
Amanda was not prepared to die
She grabbed a pencil and poked him in the eye,
Then she laughed, 'Now you may die!'

Amanda met a bumblebee
Amanda, Amanda didn't see.
The bee was small, the bee was strong,
The bee was thin and rather long.
The bee said, 'Amanda, how do you do?
Now my child I will sting you!'
Amanda, Amanda didn't cry,
Amanda wasn't prepared to die.
She reached for a swatter and smacked it across the head
Then she said, 'Now you're dead!'

Amanda met a giant slug
Amanda, Amanda knew he was a bug.
The slug was thin, the slug was round,
The slug was smelly and made a horrible sound!
The slug said, 'Amanda how do you do?
Now I will slime over you!'
Amanda, Amanda didn't cry,
Amanda wasn't prepared to die.
She grabbed some salt and sprinkled it over its head
Then she shrieked, 'I will slime you instead!'

Rachel Prescott (10)
Burscough Village Primary School

The Stampede

Jake, Jake didn't use his rake
The snake was slimy
Jake said, 'You'd better remind me.'
The snake shouted, 'You'd better run!'
Jake wanted to run to his mum.
Jake, Jake didn't lie,
Jake wasn't scared to die!
Jake, Jake got his rake
Jake, Jake killed the snake.

Jake met an enormous monkey,
He was a McDonald's junky
The monkey was nasty
He did some pasty
'How do you do Jake?
Now I will eat you.'
Jake, Jake didn't lie
Jake wasn't scared to die!
Jake, Jake gave him a cake
Then he pushed him in the lake.

Jake met an enormous bee,
Jake kicked him in the knee.
The bee was cocky,
He was called Rocky.
'Hello,' said the bee,
'Now I will sting you in the knee.'
Jake, Jake didn't lie
Jake wasn't scared to die!
Jake, Jake killed the bee,
Jake used his knee.

Jake Spencer (10)
Burscough Village Primary School

Melony's Adventures

Melony met a man-eating eel,
Melony didn't scream or squeal.
The eel was fat, the eel was hungry,
All the eel's scales were soft and spongy.
The eel said, 'Melony, how do you do?
You better run before I eat you!'
Melony, Melony wasn't shy,
Melony wasn't prepared to cry.
She sat in the corner and made a plot,
Then Melony tied the eel in a knot.

Melony met a hideous giant,
Melony didn't go shy or silent.
The giant was ugly, the giant was tall,
If you fell off his head you'd have a great fall.
The giant said, 'Melony don't try to escape,
I'll squish you when you get to the gate!'
Melony, Melony wasn't shy,
Melony wasn't prepared to cry.
She took a stick all burning and hot,
Then poked the giant on the bott.

Melony met a fluffy yeti,
Melony shouted, 'Is your name Bettie?'
The yeti was a killer, the yeti was bold,
The yeti's hair was soft and cold.
The yeti said, 'Melony, glad to meet you,
Yo ho Melony now I'll eat you.'
Melony, Melony wasn't shy,
Melony wasn't prepared to cry.
Melony took her pocket mirror,
She reflected the ice, what a chiller!

Kim Burke (10)
Burscough Village Primary School

The Adventures Of Rebecca

Rebecca met a big fat bird,
Rebecca, Rebecca was not scared.
The bird was mean, the bird was fat,
The bird was round and on a perch it sat.
The bird said, 'Rebecca, glad to meet you,
Now I'll turn you into a worm and eat you.'
Rebecca, Rebecca stood her ground,
Rebecca wasn't jumping around.
Rebecca's eyes began to flicker,
As she flashed the pistol from her knicker.

Rebecca met a robot teacher
Rebecca thought he was a preacher.
The teacher was tall, the teacher was big,
Everyone said he was a pig.
The teacher said, 'Rebecca you haven't done enough work,
I'll give you the cane for calling me a jerk.'
Rebecca, Rebecca stood her ground,
Rebecca wasn't jumping around.
Rebecca took the teacher's cane,
Rebecca, Rebecca then gave him pain.

Emma Francis (10)
Burscough Village Primary School

The Monsters Rebecca Met

Rebecca met an enormous snake,
Rebecca, Rebecca thought it was a rake.
The snake was poisonous, the snake was hungry,
The snake's big mouth was full with dungry.
The snake said, 'Rebecca, I prefer to fight you,
How do you do, now I'll bite you.'
Rebecca, Rebecca showed no tears,
And she showed no fright or fears.
She put on her gloves and straightened her hair up,
Then Rebecca quickly ate the snake up.

Rebecca saw a colourful log,
Rebecca bought a beautiful dog.
The log was colourful, the dog was fierce,
The dog's big legs were full with tears.
The log said, 'Rebecca, nice to meet you
How do you do, now I'll eat you.'
Rebecca, Rebecca showed no tears,
And she showed no fright or fears.
She thought of something very cool,
Rebecca cut the log into quarters and found one jewel.

Danielle Keogan (10)
Burscough Village Primary School

Dan Met . . .

Dan met a bunny,
He said, 'I was funny.'
The bunny was nice, the bunny was mad,
Yesterday he lost his dad.
The bunny said, 'Dan nice to meet you,
I am hungry, so I will eat you!'
Dan, Dan didn't skedaddle,
Dan stayed and won the battle.
I looked up in the sky,
And hoped the bunny would die.

Dan met a fierce lion,
So brave he ate an iron!
The lion was brave, the lion was hurt,
The collar said his name was Burt.
'Dan nice to meet you,' he said,
'Come closer and I will put you to bed.'
Dan, Dan didn't skedaddle,
Dan just stayed and won the battle.
I found an iron,
And burnt the lion!

Dan met a wriggly worm,
It even stunk and had a germ.
The worm was shocked, the worm was still,
The wriggly worm was born in a mill.
The worm said, 'Dan,
I will cook you in my pan.'
Dan, Dan didn't skedaddle,
Dan stayed and won the battle.
I flicked a germ,
And killed the worm.

Daniel Santos (11)
Burscough Village Primary School

Danielle's Adventures

Danielle met a massive snake,
Danielle, Danielle had a rake.
The snake was black, the snake had spots,
The snake had a pink frilly frock!
'Oh do come here to me.
I will bite and eat you up,' said he.
Danielle, Danielle had to lie,
Danielle didn't try to cry.
She rubbed her hands and killed a bee,
Then Danielle tied the snake to a tree!

Danielle met a crazy goose,
While she was eating a strawberry mousse.
The goose was mad, the goose had fur deep,
The goose's ducklings were all in a heap.
'You have beautiful eyes,
Now I will peck them so you'll die!'
Danielle, Danielle had to lie.
Danielle didn't try to cry.
She washed her hands and smashed a cup,
And then she calmly ate the goose up!

Danielle, Danielle met a fairy,
Danielle, Danielle called her Mary.
The fairy, who was big and hairy,
She looked incredibly scary!
'Come here Danielle give this fairy a hug,
But first I will have to turn you into a bug.'
Danielle, Danielle had to lie,
Danielle didn't try to cry.
She washed her hands and gave her a hug,
But then she turned the fairy into a bug!

Megan Elloy (10)
Burscough Village Primary School

Christopher The Brainy

Christopher met the Incredible Hulk,
Christopher, Christopher didn't sulk.
The hulk was green, the hulk was tall,
The hulk's head was very small!
The hulk said, 'Christopher eat your lunch,
After your lunch, I'll take a punch.'
Christopher, Christopher didn't know,
Christopher isn't scared of foe.
Christopher got a great big fan,
And turned him back into a normal man.

Once on a night as windy as a fan,
Christopher, Christopher met Batman.
Batman was cold, Batman was as quiet as a mouse,
He came swinging into the house.
'I'm going to get you,' he had to shout,
'Once I find you I'll knock you out.'
Christopher, Christopher didn't know,
Christopher isn't scared of foe.
Christopher pushed him out the window,
And he landed on the plant spindow.

Christopher met a swamp creature,
Christopher thought it looked like his teacher.
The swamp creature was blue,
He had red eyes gleaming too!
The swamp creature said, 'I'll eat your head,
And turn you into bread.'
Christopher, Christopher didn't know,
Christopher isn't scared of foe.
Christopher saw through the fog,
And pushed him into a muddy bog.

Sean Kelly (10)
Burscough Village Primary School

Sean's Adventures Of The Ring

Sean met an enormous cave troll,
Sean claimed the rocky knoll,
The troll was hungry, the troll was angry,
The troll's big hammer was mighty and mangly.
The troll said, 'Sean, glad to meet you,
My, my, Sean, now I'll crush you.'
Sean didn't sigh,
Sean was not afraid to die.
He cleaned his hands and gave a sharp stare,
Then, Sean quietly gave the troll a nightmare!

Sean met a cruel Orc,
Sean, Sean found an enormous fork.
The Orc was mad, the Orc was brutal,
The Orc's sharp sword was pointy and neutral.
The Orc said, 'Sean, how are you?
Now I'll kill you.'
Sean, Sean didn't sigh,
Sean was not afraid to die.
He showed no fear, he showed no rancour,
Then, Sean turned the Orc into blood and drank her.

Sean met a crazy goblin,
Sean, Sean found his friend the Moblin.
The goblin was stupid, the goblin was thick,
The goblin's longbow was heavy and sick.
The goblin said, 'Sean, how do?
Now I'll shoot you.'
Sean, Sean didn't sigh,
Sean was not afraid to die.
He nibbled the naan bread that he always fed off,
Then, Sean brutally cut the goblin's head off.

Alan Mawdsley (10)
Burscough Village Primary School

Rebecca's Enemies

Rebecca met an evil brain,
Rebecca knew it died in rain,
The brain was purple, the brain was slimy,
When the brain talked it was really swimy.
The brain said, 'Rebecca. Lovely name,
I'm going to eat you. What a shame!'
Rebecca, Rebecca didn't cry,
Rebecca wasn't scared to die.
She put on her coat and grabbed the brain,
Rebecca took it out in the rain.

Rebecca met an ugly ghoul,
The ghoul, thought Rebecca was a fool,
The ghoul was swift, the ghoul was mean,
The ghoul thought she was the Queen!
The ghoul said, 'Boo you screff,
I'm going to scare *you* half to death.'
Rebecca, Rebecca didn't cry,
Rebecca wasn't scared to die.
She quickly hoovered up the ghoul,
Then she shouted, 'Now you're the fool!'

Rebecca met a huge lion,
Rebecca, Rebecca didn't start cryin',
The lion was hungry, the lion said, 'Hello.'
The lion's sharp teeth were always yellow.
The lion growled, 'Hello Rebecca I'll have you for lunch,
I'll knock you out with just one punch!'
Rebecca, Rebecca didn't cry,
Rebecca wasn't scared to die.
She strangled the lion with a whip,
She kissed goodbye on the lion's blue lips!

Rebecca Power (10)
Burscough Village Primary School

Johnny's Adventures

Johnny met a cheeky monkey,
Johnny thought he was funky.
The monkey started ooing,
So Johnny started booing.
The monkey said, 'Johnny pleased to meet you,
Now come my boy and I'll kill you!'
Johnny, Johnny did not laugh,
Johnny didn't even act daft.
Johnny covered him in red,
Let out the bulls so he was dead.

Johnny met a fierce lion,
So he bought a hot iron.
The lion was big, the lion was bold,
The lion was ugly, the lion was old.
The lion snarled, 'Come here my chunk of meat,'
Then he snapped, 'Me fierce, me hungry, me eat!'
Johnny, Johnny did not laugh,
Johnny didn't even act daft.
Johnny threw him in the lake,
With a piece of birthday cake!

Johnny met a nasty devil,
So he played with D J Neville.
The devil was mean, the devil was scary,
His horns were big and hairy.
He pulled out a sander that was made by Bosch
'Now let me give you a nice warm bubbly wash.'
Johnny, Johnny didn't laugh,
Johnny didn't even act daft.
Johnny pulled out the holy cross,
Devil died because of not being boss!

Phillip King (11)
Burscough Village Primary School

The Adventures Of Kahu

Kahu met two fat ogres,
Kahu, Kahu drank some soda.
The ogres were hungry, the ogres were scary,
The ogres big clubs were brown and hairy.
The ogres said 'Kahu glad to meet you,
How do, Kahu, now we'll beat you!'
Kahu, Kahu didn't scare,
Kahu didn't pull o t his hair.
He washed his hands and got a stick,
And beat them until they were thick.

Kahu met a messy wizard,
Kahu, Kahu ignored the blizzard.
The wizard was big, the wizard was mean,
The wizard's magic was powerful and keen.
'Hello Kahu' said the wizard with a hug,
'Now I'll turn you into a bug.'
Kahu, Kahu, didn't scare,
Kahu didn't pull out his hair.
Kahu said 'Didlee Dee'
And turned the wizard into a tree.

Michael Boucher (11)
Burscough Village Primary School

The Adventures Of Eragon

Eragon met an elf,
Eragon carried on full of wealth.
The elf was foolish as well as cruel,
The elf battled Eragon in a duel.
Using his sword Zar'roc,
He hit the elf into a rock.
Eragon, Eragon felt his rib,
Eragon continued on his trip.
Eragon beat the foolish elf,
And now is very content with himself.

Eragon met an enormous dragon,
But he thought it was a kragon.
Eragon was scared out of his skin,
He shouted out, 'OK, you win.'
The dragon came at Eragon,
But all of a sudden he was gone.
Eragon, Eragon felt his rib,
Eragon continued on his trip.
The dragon appeared clueless,
Eragon came out scratchless.

Christopher Rice (11)
Burscough Village Primary School

Christina's Nightmare

Christina met an enormous snake,
Christina pulled her in the lake.
The snake was slimy, the snake was spotty,
The snake's fluffy neck said her name, Lottey.
The snake shouted, 'I'll grind your bones to make my bread!
I'll always do it in until you're dead!'
Christina, Christina didn't cry,
Christina didn't want to die.
Christina got up and went to the snake,
Then poked the snake's head off and went to bake!

Christina met an ugly frog,
Christina found it on the log,
The frog was ugly the frog was hairy,
The frog's collar said her name, Mary.
The frog said, 'I'll suck your blood and push you in the garden to play in the mud.'
Christina, Christina didn't cry,
Christina didn't want to die.
Christina put her in the mud,
Then went home to clean the rug!

Christina met a flying bee,
Christina thought it was a tree!
The bee was small, the bee was black,
The bee went and hid in a sack.
The bee shouted, 'Christina go away,
Come back when I am not here another day!'
Christina, Christina didn't cry,
Christina didn't want to die.
Christina got up and went to the bee,
And said, 'You really don't look like me.'

Christina Martland (10)
Burscough Village Primary School

Christina's Adventures

Christina once found a snake, the snake said, 'Hi.'
Christina said goodbye and cut off his slimy head as well as his eye.
The snake was in pain,
Christina said, 'Oh great here we go again!'
Christina, Christina could not cry,
Christina was not prepared to die!
She stood on the snake and hit it with a rake
And sent him flying down the lake.

Christina saw a giant bear
Christina was not easy to scare
She went behind a bush,
And gave him a giant push, and turned him into a horrid mush,
And she swept him under a bush.
Christina, Christina could not cry,
Christina was not prepared to die!
She waited for a gush of wind,
And threw him up and he was binned.

Christina was caught by a giant bird
Christina wasn't at all scared,
She heard the bird and she was not scared,
But his hair was really flared.
She pulled off his pants and then she was scared,
Christina, Christina could not cry,
Christina was not prepared to die!
She broke his leg and he began to beg,
'No, no please don't break my other leg.'

Simon Clegg (10)
Burscough Village Primary School

The Adventures Of Samus

Samus met a troublesome elf,
Samus simply sat on a shelf,
The elf had a bow; the elf had some arrows,
The elf's long hair was slick and narrow.
'How do Samus!' the elf shouted,
I'll chop you up and put you on a mountain!
Samus didn't use her ice gun,
Samus didn't scream or run.
She got a missile and her mace,
And sent the elf deep into space!

        Once in a palace with the sound of a ping,
        Samus met a weird king.
        The king had a sword, the king was scary,
        The king's big belly was fat and hairy.
        'Hello Samus,' said the king with a bellow,
        'I'll stab you and nab you until you're hollow!'
        Samus didn't use her ice gun,
        Samus didn't scream or run.
        She planted a bomb on the king's head,
        And then she scarpered into her shed.

Samus met a stumpy dwarf,
Samus didn't scream or hoaf.
The dwarf had a helmet, the dwarf had armour,
The dwarf had axes as big as Lamas.
'All right Samus,' the dwarf said,
'I'll grind your bones to make my bread!'
Samus didn't use her ice gun,
Samus didn't scream or run.
She rolled the dwarf into a ball,
And Samus dropped him with a great fall.

Kieran Forshaw (11)
Burscough Village Primary School

Jake's Adventures

Jake met an enormous snake
Jake, Jake wasn't fully awake.
The snake was hungry, the snake was ravenous,
The snake was cruel and cavernous.
Jake said, 'How do you do?'
The snake said, 'How do you do? Now I'll eat you.'
Jake, Jake didn't cry
Jake wasn't scared to die.
Jake got the snake
Jake killed the snake with his rake.

Jake met an enormous bug
Jake, Jake thought it was a slug.
The bug was big, green and mean
The bug's small mouth was green and mean.
The bug said, 'Glad to meet you.'
'How do you do - buggy?'
'Now I'll squish you.'
Jake, Jake didn't cry,
Jake wasn't scared to die.
Jake, Jake looked into the eye.

Jake met an enormous bee,
Jake, Jake didn't see the tree.
The bee was fat, the bee was yellow,
The bee's small stinger was sharp and shallow.
The bee said, 'Glad to meet you,
Now I'll sting you to death.'
Jake, Jake didn't cry,
Jake wasn't scared to die.
Jake, Jake, wasn't shy,
Jake squished it with a pie.

Kurtis Rothwell (9)
Burscough Village Primary School

The Adventures Of Brian

Brian met an enormous lion,
Brian, Brian started crying.
The lion was big, the lion was bold,
The lion never did as he was told.
The lion said 'Brian, glad to meet you,
Now then Brian, I'm going to eat you!'
Brian, Brian didn't worry,
Brian wasn't in a hurry.
He called the safari park and asked for help,
Then Brian waited for the lion to yelp!

Brian met an enormous bird,
Brian, Brian wasn't scared.
The bird was big, the bird was fat,
The bird wore a frilly pink hat.
'How do Brian,' the bird screamed,
'I'll drink your blood because I'm mean.'
Brian, Brian didn't worry,
Brian wasn't in a hurry.
He threw the bird in the water,
And never harmed the bird's daughter.

Christopher Watson (11)
Burscough Village Primary School

There Once Was A Teacher At School

There once was a teacher at school
Who was as stubborn as a mule.
He thought he was cool
'Til he slipped in the pool.
That silly old teacher at school!

Sam Bowker (11)
Christ Church CE School

What Should A Dragon Wear?

What should a dragon wear?
Maybe a clump of fake hair?
A really cool shirt to get all the girls
Oh what should a dragon wear?
What should a dragon say
To his mother on Valentine's Day?
'Hello Mum, Happy Valentine's'
Oh, what should a dragon say?
How should a dragon behave
When he's just bought a brand new cave?
Don't jump on the chairs or give people the scares
Oh, how should a dragon behave?
What should a dragon drive
On holiday when he arrives?
Should he buy a Ferrari and go on safari?
Oh, what should a dragon drive?

Eleanor White (11)
Christ Church CE School

Excuses

Late again Jordan!
I was messing with my hair.
Where's your homework?
Dog ate it!
Why are you wearing trainers?
'Cause my shoes are in the wash!
Why no packed lunch?
'Cause I can't make it.
Why can't you write legibly?
'Cause I trapped my hand in the door!
Why is your shirt not tucked in?
'Cause I was rushing.
Where are your glasses?
I dropped them and they're smashed.

Olivia Laycock (10)
Christ Church CE School

Cinquain

Churchyard
Gravestones in moss
For many years to come
The snowdrops cover up gravestones
Guarding!

Megan Cox (11)
Christ Church CE School

Churchyard

Churchyard
Makes me feel sad
Everytime I go
All around me are the gravestones
Silence.

Ainsley Roscoe (10)
Christ Church CE School

Snowdrops

Snowdrops
White as crystals
Spread across the churchyard
Brightening the graves.
Wonderful feelings.

Lauren Ingram (11)
Christ Church CE School

Snowdrops

Snowdrops -
The silky feel of velvet in the sun
Stand still as if nothing is there
Snowdrops.

Siôn Wells (11)
Christ Church CE School

The Teacher

There once was a teacher at school
Who thought he was really cool.
He went to Blackpool,
Where he bought a jewel,
That silly old teacher from school.

Harriet Rigby (10)
Christ Church CE School

Cinquain

Raindrops
Fall like a rock.
'Ow!' Hits me on my face.
Puddles turning into deadly
Flooding!

Jonathan Frost (11)
Christ Church CE School

Limerick

There was an old lady from Mallorca
Who got eaten up by an Orca.
Her mum wept and cried
When she heard that she'd died
That silly old lady from Mallorca.

Mason Banks (10)
Christ Church CE School

Teacher

There once was a teacher from school
Who thought he was very cool.
He kicked a stool and fell in a pool
That silly old teacher from school.

Sam Richardson (10)
Christ Church CE School

Seasons

Springtime . . .
Small lambs are born
Different flowers bloom
The birds sing very tunefully.
Spring ends.

Summer . . .
Very hot days
Flowers blaze in the sun.
It ends.
Autumn is creeping up
On us.

Eleanor Attwood-Jones (10)
Christ Church CE School

Snowdrops - Cinquain

Snowdrops -
A sign of spring.
Stand out in big green fields.
Brighten up a miserable day.
Spring comes.

Lucy Dawson (11)
Christ Church CE School

Limerick

There once was a dragon from China.
But England was even finer.
He moved over, crushed his Rover
Now that silly old dragon lives in
Dover.

Louie Turner (10)
Christ Church CE School

Churchyard Guards - Cinquain

Churchyard
Guards standing there.
In the night, in the day.
Protecting the dead is their job.
The trees.

Sam Lacey (11)
Christ Church CE School

The Tax Payer From Leeds

There was a tax payer from Leeds,
He swallowed a packet of seeds . . .
Within an hour,
His hair was a flower,
And his facial hair,
Covered in weeds!

Jordan Simpson (10)
Christ Church CE School

Rainbow

I see a rainbow -
As rain falls soft in the sky.
Sunlight touches rain,
White light touches the prism . . .
A beautiful sight it is!

Gemma Bowers (10)
Christ Church CE School

The Seasons - Cinquains

Spring comes -
The world wakes up,
Winter is now over,
Flowers growing, animals born,
Spring's here.

Summer -
The sun shines down,
On the summer lilies,
We feel the warmth on our faces.
Summer.

Autumn -
Leaves fall off trees,
Gently land on the ground.
Crunch, crunch my feet walk over them -
Dead leaves.

Winter -
Sun stops shining.
Come back don't leave us here
In this freezing cold atmosphere.
Bye sun!

Emily Potter (10)
Christ Church CE School

Cinquain

Churchyard
Dark and shadowed
Snowdrops dance in the breeze
Bare brown trees protect the gravestones
Grave guards.

Jack Dalby (10)
Christ Church CE School

Bonfire Night

As I look into the heart of the bonfire I watch my Guy Fawkes
burn into ashes.
And then I watch the rockets set off, zooming and whistling
into the sky.
I wish I could fly.

I put some wood on the fire.
The flames rose.
I heard the Jumping Jack crackling and popping.
The sparklers twinkle and splatter.
I smell food.
Now I am in a good mood.

I watch everyone's face glow as I see the sparklers shimmer.
And the Catherine wheels zoom and change colour green, blue,
yellow, purple, silver and gold.

I watch the people eat things like toffee apples, treacle toffee,
hot dogs, chips and fish.
As they all eat cakes, ice lollies, ice cream, biscuits
and jelly - yummy!

Paul Lowcock (8)
Gilded Hollins Primary School

In Someone Else's Shoes

If I wore shining armour
I would gallop through the woods
On my white horse.
I would charge through the snowiest places
To slay a ferocious dragon
And be back in time for tea.

Adam Purcell (8)
Gilded Hollins Primary School

Bonfire Night

Whizz goes the rocket in the air then a shower of glitter
in the cold dark sky.
Up goes the rocket.
There is a big bang.
There's glowing glitter flickering everywhere.

As the fireworks zoom in the air they hiss like a snake
then they roar like a lion.
*Zoom, pop, bang, crackle, crackle, crackle, bang, pop, zoom, bang
bang, pop, crackle, crackle, zoom, pop, bang.*
We have lots of bubbling cola.
Whizz go the fireworks while my cola hisses away.

Shimmer, flicker, twinkle when you shake the sparklers -
but don't forget to wear gloves.
Shimmer, glitter, zoom in the air - then a shimmer of glitter
everywhere.
Nice to look at but very noisy.

Annabelle Harrison (9)
Gilded Hollins Primary School

How The Duddon Moves Through The Valley

The Duddon River is . . .

Rushing and splashing and diving,
Crashing and turning and twisting,
Smashing and flowing and going,
Rippling and tipping and dripping,
Screaming and gleaming and shining,
Speeding and waving and roaring,
And that's how the Duddon,
Goes down to the sea.

James Hodgson (9)
Gilded Hollins Primary School

Nightwalk In Dunnerdale

The stars were like
Glittering crystals
Of moonlight.

The sound of the river
Was like a raging
Stampede.

The lights of the cars on the pass
Were like a hill
Of shooting stars.

The wind in the trees
Was like a giant
Breathing.

The lights of Hinning House
Were like blazing
Heavy beams.

Thomas Hibbert (9)
Gilded Hollins Primary School

Fireworks

Fluorescent fireworks dazzle in the dark canopy
Crackling and banging like party poppers
Forming a cacophony of sound
Twisting, turning, intertwining making incredible colours.

Silhouetted figures gape at the vivid colours
Ruby-red, sapphire-blue and vibrant orange
Race into the sky.

Sparks spit and spray then develop into nothing
Catherine wheels screech until they die
Rapid rockets zoom into the midnight sky
Luminous sparkles crackle then, fade.

Adam Pierce Jones (10)
Gilded Hollins Primary School

Fear

Fear is a predator.
It prowls at your heels
You hear its stealthy footfalls
Before it pounces.

Fear lurks in dark places -
Cold, gloomy dungeons
Where once dead bodies lay
And tortured voices cried.

Fear hides in a black tunnel
Footsteps echo off the cold stone walls
Rain drips from the jagged roof.

Fear manipulates your mind.
Like a master player
It moves you across the board and controls you.

Anya Hoque (10)
Gilded Hollins Primary School

Autumn

The autumn sky
Holds the pale, yellow sun
Which gently throws its warmth
Onto the chilly Earth.

Tall bare trees
Upset at the coming of winter
Cry bitterly,
Cascading rainbow leaves
Which flutter down
Resembling multicoloured teardrops.

A solitary bird glides
Across the empty sky
Whilst exhaled breath
Swirls and rises
Like steam from an engine.

Joseph Heaton (10)
Gilded Hollins Primary School

Amulet

Watching me are the fluffy clouds
Watching the fluffy clouds are
the soaring birds
Watching the soaring birds are
the colossal mountains
Watching the colossal mountains
is the dark green forest
Watching the dark green forest
are two stony faces
Watching the two stony faces is
the calm wind
Watching the calm wind are the
huge stone boulders
Watching the huge stone boulders
is me
Watching me are the fluffy
clouds.

Joshua Wilcock (9)
Gilded Hollins Primary School

Fear

Fear is like a lion
Its bright eyes glaring through the dark
Getting ready to
Pounce on you
In the heart of a forest.

Fear, like a swarm of ants,
Scatters in your mind
Hiding in pitch-black corners.

Fear lurks in dark dungeons,
In a silent graveyard where
Only the wind is heard
Echoing in your mind.

Daniel Mason (9)
Gilded Hollins Primary School

Nightwalk In Dunnerdale

The branches of the trees
Were like
Endless hands.

The stars were
Like sparkling
Crystals.

The wind in the trees was like
A fox stalking
Its prey.

The clouds in the sky
Look like bird wings.

The light under the cloud
Was like a faint fire.

The lights of Hinning House
Looked like
Sparkling jewels.

Daniel Wood (9)
Gilded Hollins Primary School

Fear

Fear lurks in a dark tunnel
Water drips from the ceiling
Footsteps creep behind you
Whispers fill your ears.

Behind the wardrobe
Under the bed
Waiting until after midnight
Waiting to creep out.

Fear is a wolf
Howling in the dark
Echoing in your brain
Sending shivers down your spine.

Jareth Turner (10)
Gilded Hollins Primary School

Fireworks

Bang!
A thunderous rocket races
High into the blackness
Erupting into myriads of cascading diamonds
Illuminating the sky
Fading and dying.

Pots of multicoloured glitter
Are spilled randomly
Across the velvet canopy
Zingy-red golden dazzle and hot ginger
Performing a hypnotic dance.

Sparklers
Gleaming into the night sky
Many patterns, different colours,
Flame reds, electric blues and tropical limes
Burst into iridescent sparkles.

Matthew Royle (9)
Gilded Hollins Primary School

Autumn Days

White candyfloss clouds
Gently swirl
In the pale blue sky.

Leafless bushes
Support oval red berries
Which hang like sparkling rubies.

A veil of white mist
Hangs in the air
Gradually disappearing
In the pale yellow sunshine.

Delicate cobwebs
Cloaked with shining drops of dew
Glisten like crystals.

Bethany Bramall (9)
Gilded Hollins Primary School

Cathedral Cave

The wall of the tunnel
was like a cat's rough tongue,
on your fingers.

The clatter of the stones
Was like wine glasses
Clashing together.

The entrance of the cave
Was like a huge shark's mouth
Full of white teeth.

The pillar of the cave
Was like a giant slithering
Green snake.

The water in the cave
Was like a
Glistening, glass mirror.

Milo Pendlebury (9)
Gilded Hollins Primary School

A Summer Poem

A crest-blue sky
covered with candyfloss clouds
supports the shining sun.
Birds sing in the tall trees.

As a gentle breeze whispers in my ear
while leaves give shade to a bird like a parasol
defending it from the sun.

Colourful leaves sway
while hanging from an ancient branch
on a tall aged tree.
A blackberry bush snakes through the undergrowth
whilst tempting birds to a scrumptious feast.

Emma Seddon (10)
Gilded Hollins Primary School

Nightwalk In Dunnerdale

The branches of the tree
were like a lion's
claws.

The stars hung
like lanterns.

The shape of the mountain
looked like big, billowing
clouds.

Walking across the bog
was like walking on wet sand.

The lights of Hinning House
were glistening
like diamonds.

Jessica Bolton (10)
Gilded Hollins Primary School

Chimney Sweep

Scared
Sad
Alone
Microscopic dust
Forces me to cough and splutter.
It sticks to my dry throat.
My whole body aches
Trapped in a lonely black prison.

In a blue circle of sky
A bird flies freely
Giving me faith.

Rosie Willis (10)
Gilded Hollins Primary School

Amulet

The rippling lake synchronises the dappled colours of
lights in Coniston Village.
Coniston Village is sheltered
by the sleeping trees.
The sleeping trees shed their leaves
carpeting the ground in vibrant shades of autumn.
The vibrant shades of autumn crunch underfoot.
Underfoot the beams of our torches
dance dreamily
like miniature stars parading across the satin sky.
The satin sky reflects the vastness of the universe.
The vastness of the universe
plunges through the misty darkness
and dives into the tranquillity of the rippling lake.
The rippling lake synchronises the dappled colours
of the lights in Coniston Village.

Alex Miller (10)
Gilded Hollins Primary School

Amulet

The clear water listens to the spiky trees
The spiky trees listen to the noisy wind
The noisy wind listens to the rough stones
The rough stones listen to the long grass
The long grass listens to the huge mountain
The huge mountain listens to the pale sky
The pale sky listens to the winding river
The winding river listens to the smooth stone wall
The smooth stone wall listens to the clear water.

Lucy Woodcock (9)
Gilded Hollins Primary School

Winter Poem

Crystallised trees
shimmer
in the pale winter sunlight.

Cobwebs sparkle
like fine silver thread
festooning gates and hedgerows.

A patchwork carpet of decaying leaves
glistens
in the early rays of the sun.

The frozen lake
is coated
by a layer of sieved snow
like sprinkled icing sugar
on a cake.

Nicola Goulden (10)
Gilded Hollins Primary School

Fear

Fear is like a shark
as it swims through the deep
and snaps his jaws ready to eat.

Fear is like a swarm of bees
ready to sting
and insert its poison.

Fear lurks in your brain
speeding through like blood in your veins
and manipulating your mind.

Alexandra Larkin (10)
Gilded Hollins Primary School

Chimney Sweep

Trapped
in a roller-coaster tunnel,
smothered
by black suffocating soot.
The sun's rays penetrate,
the darkness.
Shooting pain
rushes through my leg
as it scrapes the sharp bricks.
Echoing screams,
Angry shouts.
Bitter wind
whirls through me,
Trapped
in a roller-coaster tunnel.

Sally Boardman (11)
Gilded Hollins Primary School

A Summer Poem

Freshly cut grass
Smells like smoky bacon
While the sun's hot rays
Pierce the canopy of green leaves
Lacerated with holes
Made by a hungry caterpillar.

The deep blue sky
Splashed with translucent,
Fluffy white clouds
Envelops a glittering aeroplane.

Alex Cordery (10)
Gilded Hollins Primary School

Amulet

The glistening lake captures the gleaming lights of
Coniston Village.
Coniston Village is lost in the ebony mountains.
The ebony mountains are silhouetted against the
monotonous sky.
The monotonous sky comes to life with the
twinkling stars.
The twinkling stars dance in the glistening lake.
The glistening lake captures the gleaming lights of
Coniston Village.

Adam King (11)
Gilded Hollins Primary School

Amulet

Silver stars play dot-to-dot
in the midnight sky.
In the midnight sky,
the moon shines on the rippling lake.
The rippling lake caresses
Coniston Beach.
Coniston Beach is protected by the mountains.
The mountains turn their faces
to the silver stars
Silver stars play dot-to-dot
in the midnight sky.

Georgia Overend (10)
Gilded Hollins Primary School

Rock Scrambling

Noisy,
Excited.
Gushing water crashes violently
against the slippery rocks
like a pounding dog.
The cascading waterfall
plunges against nature
eroding a foaming pool
eagerly jumping from rock to
rock,
hoping to go on forever.
The greatest activity of all!

Daniel Lynch (10)
Gilded Hollins Primary School

Chimney Sweeps

Tired
Helpless
Cold
Pain and anger are suppressed inside me
Like a bottle waiting to explode.
Soot hovers like a cobra ready to strike
at my helpless lungs.
Light at the end of the tunnel
tantalises me
As I pray for my nightmare to end.

Daniel Kidd (11)
Gilded Hollins Primary School

Night Falls Over Coniston

The stars sparkle like glitter dropped on a
black silken sheet.
The moon glows like a silver circle glued to the
night sky.
Silhouettes of trees dance in the gentle breeze.
On the jetty tea-lights float in the water.
Multicoloured towers of Coniston village
are reflected in the rippling lake
like spilt paint on a black piece of paper.
The windows of the boat house splinter
the moonlight.

Amy Wilcock (10)
Gilded Hollins Primary School

Night Falls Over Coniston

Jagged mountains tower over
the glazed lake.
Shimmering stars catch the silvery light
like a crystal chandelier.
The lake's surface ripples
like an infinite whisper.
The shriek of an owl
disturbs the silence
like a wolf crying for its pack.
Cold crawls like an icy spider
through my skin.

Charlotte Monaghan (10)
Gilded Hollins Primary School

In Someone Else's Shoes

The final countdown
Blast Off!
The monster machine breaks free from its vibrating restraints
And zooms upward into the atmosphere
At 28,000 miles per hour
Moments later
I'm cruising through an immense black abyss
Surrounded by millions
Of tiny, sparkling stars
And the Earth
Is a blue marbled sphere
Embedded in the centre of the ominous black night
My heart beats 200 times a minute
As the landing module descends to the moon's surface
A cushioned bump
The module door hatch automatically opens
Revealing the silvery dusty surface of the moon
Taking the first step on another planet
One small step for a man
One giant leap for mankind.

Thomas Walsh (11)
Gilded Hollins Primary School

Night Falls Over Coniston

A silken spider's web of glowing stars
Strangles the night sky.
The misty moon hides behind the
Silhouetted mountains.
The lights of Coniston Village,
Like flickering candles,
Are reflected in the mirrored surface.
The dark depths of the lake
Conjure the myriads of stars
Floating in the sleeping sky.

Sam Blower (11)
Gilded Hollins Primary School

Water

Water is a shiny,
blue, puddle.
Water is a soggy,
wet raindrop.
Water is a dirty dark pond.
Water is a glistening, sparkling
waterfall.
Water is a shimmering, lashing
stream.
Water is a dazzling, showering, river.
Water is a shiny, calm, ocean.
Water is a deep wide sea.
Water is a crashing, floating lake.
Water is a fizzy, still reservoir.
Water is a twirling, twisting, canal.
Water is a silvery, shimmering puddle.
Water is a beautiful clear waterfall.
Water is a twisting squirting ocean water.

Hannah Rothwell (8)
Lordsgate Township CE Primary School

All About Me!

N is for noisy, I'm always so loud.
A is annoying my brother.
O is for owing my sister a pound
M is for moaning on at my mother
I is for impish but cute as can be
   - put it all together and that makes me.

Naomi Maher (9)
Lordsgate Township CE Primary School

A Spook In The Night

I got a spook in the night,
I thought I heard a ghost,
The door creaked,
The window bashed,
But the gate was noisy the most.

I got under my covers and huddled so tight,
I was beginning to get afraid of the night.
Was it a spook or my big brother,
I opened my eyes and saw my mother.

It wasn't a spook but just my mum,
She wiped my brow,
I went back to sleep, but I don't know how.

Eleanor McCombe (9)
Lordsgate Township CE Primary School

Water!

Water is a clear, shimmering puddle.
Water is a silvery, clear raindrop.
Water is a huge, beautiful pond.
Water is a crushing, dangerous waterfall.
Water is a blue, deep river.
Water is a roaring, raving ocean.
Water is a wide, cool sea.
Water is a massive, murky lake.
Water is a long-lasting reservoir.

Shimmering, flowing, cool, blue, beautiful,
Crushing, huge, raving, twisting, massive
Long-lasting
   Water!

Elliott Howarth (8)
Lordsgate Township CE Primary School

My Friend Alice

My friend has brown pony tails
My friend has two blue twinkling eyes.
My friend has a woolly red school jumper.
My friend has a small white polo shirt.
My friend has one grey skirt.
My friend has two black shiny shoes.
My friend is Alice.

Alice is very, very kind
Alice has a lovely bedroom.
Alice walks slowly
Alice talks softly.
Alice wears small-framed glasses.
Alice reads quickly.
Alice is my best friend!

Jessica Walsh (8)
Lordsgate Township CE Primary School

Big Cars, Small Cars

Big cars, small cars,
Cars in-between
All different cars
From BMWs to Fords
The world is full of them all.
So join in.
Fast cars, slow cars,
Go fast, go slow.
Cars are excellent.
Vauxhall Astras to Ferrari X4s
Join in and have some fun.

Aaron Kendall (9)
Lordsgate Township CE Primary School

My Pet Budgie

My budgie is light blue
and always flutters about
and when we let it out it always pecks about.
My budgie is a nuisance and
it always chirps about.
My budgie is so strange because
it drinks from a bath.
My budgie likes its food and water
it likes its little ladder my budgie
splashes in his bath and it likes
swinging on his swing and when
you put some food in the cage
it always pecks about.

Rebecca Pickering (9)
Lordsgate Township CE Primary School

The Little Steam Train

Faster, faster, the train will go,
Over the hill and through the snow.
Through the tunnel the animals will be,
Loads of children I can see.

Past the mountain there's a stream.
Here am I in the train with loads of steam.
There's a lion in all its glory,
Telling his cubs a story.
Faster, faster the train will always go.
Over the hill then through the snow.

Sean Smith (9)
Lordsgate Township CE Primary School

Small Cars, Big Cars

Small cars, big cars, going as fast as they can,
Small cars, big cars, BMW if they can.
Small cars, big cars, Fords as well,
Small cars, big cars some that are too small.
Small cars, big cars, some that glow,
And some that are too slow.

Steven Dawson (9)
Lordsgate Township CE Primary School

The Beach

At the beach everyone eats and sleeps
But the children have a candy bar each
The dogs bark in the sea
The sharks stay still
Staring at the strangers going by.

Bethany Graves (10)
Lordsgate Township CE Primary School

Sleeping

Fast asleep all snug in bed,
Closed the curtains like Mum said,
Turned the light off.
All is dark.

Danielle Hayman (7)
Lordsgate Township CE Primary School

When I Grow Old

I'll be a hip hop Granny and I'll dance in the street,
Stealing comics and ice cream and yummy tummy sweets.
I'll yell at the neighbours going past in their cars,
And I'll steal little children's chocolate bars.
I'll never go to work but I'll stay at home,
Yelling at my daughters on my mobile phone!

Kathryn Bridgeman (10)
Roby Mill CE Primary School

Wrestlers

Neck-breakers
Rope-jumpers
Bone-crushers
Fist-punchers
Chair-whackers
Arm-snappers
Finishing-specials.

Isaac Bradley (9)
Roby Mill CE Primary School

Yuck!

Yuck! There's a mothball
on my wall.

Yuck! There's a fish
in my dish.

Yuck! There's a dog hair
in my pear.

    Yuck!

Jordan Scully (11)
Roby Mill CE Primary School

Old Jane

She goes to the shops every day,
Buys fashionable clothes and never pays.
She eats chocolate mince pies,
And McDonalds fries.

She is as fat as a pig,
And doesn't care a fig.
Never looks like old rags,
Like other old bags

And that is the poem about Jane, the pain.

Josceline Halsall (10)
Roby Mill CE Primary School

Tarantulas - Kennings

Web spinners
Little crawlers
Poisonous biters
Venom shooters
Nightmare makers.

Nicola Bradley (9)
Roby Mill CE Primary School

TV - Kennings

Noise maker,
Children lover,
Story teller,
Family member,
Show off.

Laura Burton (11)
Roby Mill CE Primary School

The Silly Song

Jim jam, jabba, jou
Sim, sam, silly, sue
Bim, bam, babba, bong
This is a silly song.
Rim, ram, rabba, rom
Tim, tam, tabby, tom
Mim, mam, maggie, mong
This is the end of the silly song!

Tom Aitchison (9)
Roby Mill CE Primary School

The Cute Little Dog

There once was a cute little dog
And the little dog ate like a hog
He ate a big hat
Followed by a cat
And ended up gobbling a frog!

Melissa Hale (9)
Roby Mill CE Primary School

Car

There once was a really fast car
The man in it drove to a bar
He had too much drink
And was sick in the sink
And he also crashed his fast car.

James Carrington (9)
Roby Mill CE Primary School

I Hate Being Old!

I hate being old!
Having to bake
Cakes and biscuits,
Day after day after day.

I hate being old!
Always receiving
Dried apricots and prunes
On numerous birthdays.

I hate being old!
Being unable
To wear dresses
That I did long ago.

I hate being old!
Shuffling around,
Clutching a walking stick,
In an old people's home.

Eleanor Swire (11)
Roby Mill CE Primary School

My Ballerina

My ballerina has . . .
A body like a vine tomato
Eyes like pearly white diamonds
A nose like a plum stone
A mouth like a bent pencil.

My ballerina is . . .
As friendly as the happiest of all dogs
As clever as a circus clown in action
As loud as a feather dropping on the ground
As smelly as a rose in full bloom
As frightening as a little fish.

Rachel Appleton (8)
Roby Mill CE Primary School

The Girl Called France

There was a girl called France
Who loved to sing and dance
She danced on the ice
And twirled around twice
Then fell and split her pants.

Jasmine Turner (8)
Roby Mill CE Primary School

Dog

My dog has . . .
Eyes like deep, dark chocolate
A nose like a shiny, black pebble
A mouth like a dry desert
And legs like brown, skinny sticks.

Winston Halsall (7)
Roby Mill CE Primary School

Lance

There was a young boy from France
Whose real name was Lance
He chucked his lasso
And shouted yahoo
As it caught someone in dance.

Drew Winstanley (8)
Roby Mill CE Primary School

Robin

There was a robin
Who went apple bobbin'
Then went sobbin'
To his mummy robin.

Patrick Green (11)
Roby Mill CE Primary School

I Will Never Like To Be Old

I will never like to be old
To always wake up and find that I am cold
I'll have aches and pains
With bright red veins.
I will never like to be old
My house will be full of mould
My hair will go all grey
My eyes will flinch day after day
I would never ever like to be old!

Camilla Turner (11)
Roby Mill CE Primary School

Limerick

There was once a fat old man
Who always had a fake tan
He liked to sit in the sun
And bake like a bun
And that is how the story ran!

Laura Swire (8)
Roby Mill CE Primary School

Snow!

I wonder what it is like to be
A snowman?
White and fluffy,
Cold and white,
Frosty and snowy,
With big stone eyes,
And a carrot for my nose.
I wondor, I wonder
When I am lying in the snow?

Martina Kiernan (11)
St Hugh's CE Primary School, Oldham

Winter Frost

Jack Frost and his frosty dog,
Wrap up warm,
Hope that he doesn't give you *frostbite*,
If you see him, run,
Before he freezes you,
Into ice cubes,
To cool his day,
Wait for the sun to come out,
He will melt and go away.

Frank Ross (10)
St Hugh's CE Primary School, Oldham

Summer Is Here

Summer is here, the day is bright and hot
Winter has been so long that I almost forgot
The fun and the laughter
Then getting dried after
Paddling in the stream
But then I woke up and it was all a big dream
It was mid-winter and how I wished
For those hazy summer nights
When we sat upon the hillside
And watched those twinkling lights.

Jordan Senior (10)
St Hugh's CE Primary School, Oldham

Summer Poem

Summer is fun
When you're out in the sun
It gets you hot
'Til you lose the plot
When it gets so hot you begin to scream
You bury your head in some nice ice cream.

Kieron Bland (10)
St Hugh's CE Primary School, Oldham

Winter's Here!

Winter's here it's time for snow,
snowball fights, the children glow.
Freezing hands, and freezing toes,
bright red ears and nose.
The snow falls faster
big white flakes,
got to go home now, I've got the shakes.
When tomorrow comes, I'll wrap up warm,
Tonight's weather forecast says
Snowstorm!

Chloe Clarke (9)
St Hugh's CE Primary School, Oldham

The Weather

The wind whistles like a bird,
The rain drips like a tap,
The sun shines like a lamp,
The snow turns into slush,
The fog turns into mist,
The hail turns into water,
The weather is our friend.

Laura Worrall (11)
St Hugh's CE Primary School, Oldham

The Weather

The rain is like the tears that drop from your eyes.
The hail is like the water from the shower.
The snow is like the ice in the freezer.
The frost is like silver paint scattered on the floor.
The sun is so bright, it's like a bright yellow flower.
The wind is so strong, it's like a hurricane.

Charlotte Marsden (11)
St Hugh's CE Primary School, Oldham

Summertime

In the summertime,
Beauty is the sunshine.
When the rivers start to flow,
And the heat begins to soar.
Birds start to sing,
And wasps come out to sting.
Children go out to play,
In the heat all day.
Where the sun's a burning jewel,
And people try to stay cool.
Air begins to roar from a fan,
It's a time to get a tan.
Summer is when the sun is bright,
So the children fly a kite.
So that's the summertime,
And I like it just fine!

Jessica Bird (10)
St Hugh's CE Primary School, Oldham

All Things Around The World

Mad, mad as a teacher,
Kind, kind as a granny,
Helpful, helpful as a headteacher,
Cool, cool as a dude,
Bad, bad as a vandaliser,
Careful, careful as a mum and dad,
Good, good as a good girl,
Funny, funny as a joke book,
Skilful, skilful as a footballer,
Scary, scary as a dog,
Clever, clever as a mathematician,
Big, big as a giant.

Daniel Lord (9)
St Hugh's CE Primary School, Oldham

A Fright In The Night

The cat and the rat came out to play,
But the snake also had something to say,
The cat went left,
The rat went right,
And the snake went chasing them into the night.
They both ran as fast as they could,
They wanted to hide amongst the wood,
The cat jumped up a tree so tall,
The rat looked up and squeaked
'Watch you don't fall.'
The rat sat very still in the long grass,
And waited quietly for the snake to pass.
The snake slithered across the mud,
But soon after the snake heard a thud,
In the count of three, the snake caught a flea,
And the cat and the rat ran home together,
But the snake chased them all the way.

Sarah Ryder (8)
St Hugh's CE Primary School, Oldham

The Seasons

Autumn is the season for me, full of all the leaves.
A different leaf, from a different year, off a different tree.
All the children playing, throwing leaves in the air,
While adults walk down the street, crunching leaves under their feet.
Then autumn turns to winter, the coldest season of the year,
Sprinkles of snow all over the place, making everything white.
Children have more games to play, creating giant snowmen.
Sleighing down the hills and throwing lots of snowballs.
Then spring blossoms out and all the flowers grow,
Spring is sometimes rainy but gets warmer near the end.
Getting warmer and warmer by the day,
And the seasons move on to summer,
This happens every year, this is all four seasons.

Michael Doyle (11)
St Hugh's CE Primary School, Oldham

The Hulk Poem

He is green,
He can jump far,
He is strong,
He is called the Hulk!

He is big, green and very mean.
You don't want to make him go
Big.
You want to calm him down
And you will be OK.

Liam Welsh (9)
St Hugh's CE Primary School, Oldham

My Sea Poem

Crashing upon the bright golden yellow sand.
The sea is peaceful.
But when it crashes it is noisy.
If you look at the sea it is see-through.
The sea is enormous, huge as well.
When you put your boat on, it is wavy.
The mermaids and fish sing at you like a lullaby
And jump at you happily.

Rebecca Bird (8)
St Hugh's CE Primary School, Oldham

Animals And Food

Dogs are nice,
Cats are lovely,
Hamsters are good,
Chinchillas look like rabbits,
Rabbits eat carrots,
Monkeys eat bananas,
Cats eat cat food,
Dogs eat dog food.

Andrew Lomas (8)
St Hugh's CE Primary School, Oldham

Teaching

My teacher teaches in a school!
She works and plays!
She makes things and wakes things!
She sits and picks her feet!
She hides and sighs!
She huffs and puffs!
She's skinny and minny
She is tall and as thick as a wall.

Natalie Wardle (8)
St Hugh's CE Primary School, Oldham

Cats

Cats are hairy and furry
Cats are bad
They can be silly
They can be ginger
Cats can be lazy
They can be funny
They are kind
Cats are all different
But they don't mind.

Emma Henderson (8)
St Hugh's CE Primary School, Oldham

My Dog Is Loud

My dog barks at people when they knock
On the door
And walk past.
My dog is crazy and crafty.
My dog is loud
My dog likes playing with footballs
She runs around in circles.

Ashley Stewart (8)
St Hugh's CE Primary School, Oldham

All Different Things

Noise - what is noise?
Is noise, noise?
Are we noise?
Is music noise?
Who knows?
I do!

Animals - what are animals?
Are animals, animals?
Are we animals?
Who knows?
I do!

People - what are people?
Are people, people?
Are we people?
Who knows?
I do!

Pictures - what are pictures?
Are pictures, pictures?
Are we pictures?
Who knows?
I do!

Creation - what is creation?
Is creation, creation?
Are we creation?
Who knows?
I do!

The answer to all of these
You'll soon find out,
Ask your teacher,
Or look about.

Candice Jones (10)
St Hugh's CE Primary School, Oldham

At The Zoo

At the zoo, I saw a tiger,
It said on a sign, it's name was Elizer.
At the zoo, I saw a monkey,
I wish it could dance then it would be funky.
At the zoo, I saw a giraffe,
I wish it was funny, it would make me laugh.
At the zoo, I saw a chimp,
It had a broken leg, so it had to limp.
At the zoo, I saw a cub,
It could have fitted in a tub.
At the zoo, I saw a lioness,
It's a girl, like a lovely goddess.
At the zoo, I saw a lion,
I wish that it could iron.
At the zoo I saw some koalas,
I wish they were called Karas.
At the zoo I saw a beaver,
I was calling, it's pulling on a lever
And that's my day at the zoo.

Rebecca Holland (8)
St Hugh's CE Primary School, Oldham

Harry Potter's Lizard

Harry Potter is a wizard,
He tried a spell on a lizard.
He turned it blue, it said *'Achoo'*
But it didn't have a clue.
Because it was only a lizard.
The lizard was very fat,
It sat on Harry Potter's mat.
Harry was very upset,
He said 'Go on now, go, go, get.'
So the lizard slumped along,
And decided to live in a pond.

Bethany Shackleton (10)
St Hugh's CE Primary School, Oldham

About Animals

Dogs live in beds
Fish live in tanks
Hamsters live in cages
Birds live in cages too
Dogs eat dog food
Fish eat flakes
Hamsters eat fruit
Birds eat seeds
I love animals
They are lovely
They are the best.

Rebecca Cooper (8)
St Hugh's CE Primary School, Oldham

My Chess Poem

Chess is good.
Chess is mint.
Class chess.
World chess.

Magnet chess.
Chess is black and white.
Playing chess.
Little chess pieces.
Big chess pieces.
Fun chess.

Brandon Clifton (8)
St Hugh's CE Primary School, Oldham

Alton Towers

Alton Towers,
Alton Towers,
It's got so much powers,
There's not many towers,
But still it's got flowers.

As you stand on one ride,
You feel like a tide,
You often find,
That other people are kind.

You can go up and down on a very fast boat,
But make sure you're wearing your waterproof coat.
Your scream gets stuck at the back of your throat,
But at home time remember your waterproof coat.

Gabrielle Miller-Crook (10)
St James' CE Primary School, Chorley

Food

Food, food, marvellous food,
It puts me in a very good mood.
I like eating lots of chips,
I don't like eating apple pips.

I like eating Brussel sprouts,
I hate when my daddy shouts.
I adore eating sausages,
I hate eating greengages.

I like munching roasted pork
I always eat with a knife and fork.
I like eating lovely food,
It puts me in a very good mood.

Philip Jolly (10)
St James' CE Primary School, Chorley

I Hate Pancakes

I like lots of things,
Basketball and fairies' wings.
But the thing I like the best,
It's better than all the rest.
It's pancakes, pancakes, pancakes,
To this Mum says, 'For goodness sake!'

This is because of what I've just told you,
Isn't quite so very true.
When it is this Tuesday
I ignore all they say,
So I like lots of things
Basketball and fairies' wings!

Eleanor Hargreaves (11)
St James' CE Primary School, Chorley

I Like Lots Of Things

I like lots of things
Kerry is one of them,
She sings along to Atomic Kitten
As her husband sings with the Westlife band.

Kerry won 'I am a Celebrity'
She is brave, she must be.

Kerry has two children, Lilly and Molly,
Lilly and Molly.

Kerry had greatest hits, number one
She sang 'Whole Again.'

I think she is number one.

Vicky Charnley (10)
St James' CE Primary School, Chorley

Jason Robinson

J is for Jason my favourite player
A is for attention when he kicks the ball
S is for sure that he is going to win
O is for opposition when they boo and sing
N is for nasty when the crowds hiss.

R is for rugby my favourite sport
O is for opposition when they cry
B is for best that's what Jason is now.
I is for intelligence when he aims the ball
N is for nasty when the team hiss.
S is for sure he'll do his best
O is for overjoyed when we win
N is for nasty when the foes hiss.

Jake Sloan (10)
St James' CE Primary School, Chorley

Things I Like

I like chocolate, it is great,
We get it from the summer fete.
It is sweet and creamy too,
And I like it as much as you.

I like sweets they are fun,
I love to eat them yum, yum, yum.
Eat them, keep them, you can't beat them.
I love sweets, they are fun,
I like to eat them, yum, yum, yum.

I like candy, it is good,
I love to eat it with my pud.
I like to have it for my dinner,
And let my wrappers flow down the river.

Olivia Facer (10)
St James' CE Primary School, Chorley

Shout Cameron!

Who's the boy with the groovy smile
Trying to rip up my file
Holds my hand all the while
Shout Cameron, shout Cameron.
Chubby cheeks, light brown hair,
Never, never gave him a scare.
Oh yeah!
Shout Cameron, shout Cameron,
Who's the boy with all the toys?
Always plays with other boys.
Shout Cameron, shout Cameron,
Smiles at me all the time,
Even though I am nine.
I love him!
Even though he makes a din,
Shout Cameron, shout Cameron.

Joanna Price (9)
St James' CE Primary School, Chorley

Shopping

Shopping is the best, best, best,
Better than all the rest.
I always shop for shoes, shoes, shoes,
But never ever booze.
I'm always going to town, town, town,
You'll never see me frown.
My sister loves HMV, V, V,
But my mum likes Laura Ashley.
When I'm shopping for food, food, food,
I'll definitely be in a mood.

Katie Parker (11)
St James' CE Primary School, Chorley

My Best Friends

I have two best friends
Called Keri and Zoe
They sleep at my house
Every fortnight.

Even though they
Make a mess they
Will always be the best
They always beg to come
To mine.

When Keri comes to mine
She always makes me feel fine.

When Zoe comes to mine
She always makes me look at
The time.

When I have a little bath
They will always make me laugh.

Jessica Edwards (9)
St John's CE Primary School, Burscough

My Grandad

My grandad likes gardening and growing veg
He's a banana, always tanned.

One of his eyes is blind, he's going a little bit deaf.
But we still love him.
He's a jacket potato, a bit wrinkled too,
His Newcastle accent is a part of him.

Whenever I see him he's there saying 'Hello Em'
And when he's gone, he'll always be in my heart.

Emma Aldred (9)
St John's CE Primary School, Burscough

Inside A Soul

Inside a soul lives a million secrets
A river of feelings flowing through
A thump of a heart pounding fast
The cry of a thousand sorrows.

The feel of summer springing through
The laughter from the child playing free
The shiver from the child who freezes in the cold
The feel from fire upon cold hands.

A soul is a delicate thing
It lives in everyone
But only one thing is the same
That is that . . .
They all need a home
And there's a home in everyone.

Laura Wilkinson (10)
St John's CE Primary School, Burscough

My Grandma

My grandma makes cakes
the best in the world they are,
she can make ginger cake,
the best by far,
but all the same, the others are good
at Hallowe'en people came to the house and threw mud
but does it matter, she just washed it off
when I was last there I saw a rare moth.

Adam Nelson (10)
St John's CE Primary School, Burscough

Gymnastics

Gymnastics, the sport I do
Tumbling and flicking all day through.

Gymnastics, the sport for me
On the bars swinging free.

Gymnastics, the sport I love
Spectators watching from above.

Gymnastics, me on the beam
Now that is a sight to be seen!

Gymnastics, on the vault
Leaping over without a fault.

Gymnastics is great fun
Now I've finally got Badge One!

Gymnastics
Is
Fantastic!

Melissa Jones (9)
St John's CE Primary School, Burscough

The Witch's Tear

The witch's tear,
Is crystal clear.
In the moonlight,
It glows very bright.
The tear is as clear as glass,
But never will tarnish like brass.
It shines when the sun's on it,
But won't break when it gets hit.
It's as beautiful as a crystal,
But won't smash with a zap of a pistol.
It's as precious as a piece of gold.
It's so exquisite it could never be sold.

Isabel Bryant (8)
St John's CE Primary School, Burscough

Friends!

Friends are not people who come and go any time they like
Friends are not people you have to play with every day.

Friends don't just have to live round the corner
You can still be friends no matter what.

The thing I don't know is why they come and go
And that's just the way they are.

If I was them I would try to be their friend
For as long as I possibly could.

Why, oh why, do they go off on you, that's just what I hate
They stare and stare till you have to look away.

They invite you round for a sleepover
And then you don't talk the next day.

Then you say hi, and look till they reply
They smile at you then quickly turn away out of your sight.

Then you meet at the end of the street
And that's when you have your final talk.

      And that's when you become best
      Friends!

Zoe Davies (9)
St John's CE Primary School, Burscough

Cats

Cats purr while whiskers twitch
A pink nose wiggles, ears prick
Green eyes widen, tail flicks
Legs up straight body stretched
Then he leaps to catch his prey.

Helena Jamieson (9)
St John's CE Primary School, Burscough

Beware Of The Witch

Witches, witches
They're so, so mean
You better beware or you might just scream.

Witches, witches,
They're so, so mean
You might want to prepare for a big, big scare.

Witches, witches
They're so, so mean
You don't want to die by a spiteful witch.

Witches, witches
They're so, so mean
Hurry up or you might just scream.

Argh!

Rebecca Griggs (9)
St John's CE Primary School, Burscough

My Friend Kayleigh

My friend Kayleigh
has long black hair,
My friend Kayleigh
dances like she does not care.
My friend Kayleigh
has bright pink lips
My friend Kayleigh
always swallows pips.

Zoe Winders (9)
St John's CE Primary School, Burscough

In My Purple Purse

In my purple purse I will put:

The ripple of a rushing river,
The scent of spring buds,
A beat of my hammering heart.

In my purple purse I will put:

The last snort of a wild warthog,
A bomb exploding in Paris,
A note sang in a high-pitched voice.

In my purple purse I will put:

The scale of a rainbowfish,
A bubble from a bar of soap,
A squeak from a Gerbil.

In my purple purse I will put:

A feather from a sparrow,
The juice from a plumpy plump,
The spark from a flaming firework.

Joanna Lowe (9)
St John's CE Primary School, Burscough

Uncle Ronnie

Uncle Ronnie makes me laugh
He cheers me up when I am sad.
Uncle Ronnie is lots of fun
And his smile is like the sun.
Uncle Ronnie tickles me and I wriggle
He tells me a joke and I giggle.

That's Uncle Ronnie.

Sarah Woods (9)
St John's CE Primary School, Burscough

In My Magic Cauldron

In my magic cauldron I will put . . .
Sparkle of my teacher's eye,
A robber that will come and spy,
A bird, which cannot fly,
And a baby that will cry.

In my magic cauldron I will put . . .
A flutter of a fairy's broken wing,
A quince which will always sing,
A colourful firework, which brightens up the night
And a monster that has a terrible sight.

In my magic cauldron I will put . . .
A leaking blue pen,
A brown cooking hen,
A big cave den,
And a big number ten.

Mix it up and make it nice but when it turns out
It looks like rice.

Rebecca Moseley (9)
St John's CE Primary School, Burscough

Winter

The chill air blows in gusts,
freezing everything in its path.
The silent flock stand motionless,
whilst the owl hoots stiffly.

Houses close their eyes to shut out the cold
and the robin huddles up in its warm cosy nest.
The clock ticks quietly and slowly,
breaking the silence of this bitterly cold evening.

The bare bushes sway in time with the wind,
their sleep as yet unbroken.
No human movement disturbs the silence,
Nature's course remains unspoilt

Annie McLoughlin (10)
St John's CE Primary School, Burscough

The British Weather

I'm trying to figure why I feel so sad
Is it because the weather's so bad?
The rain is falling like stair-rods
It comes down like cats and dogs
The whistling wind and thunder clattering
And a lick of lightning has people scattering.

But the British weather isn't always so
I sometimes feel a warming glow
That comes from playing in the snow
This is the time when slay bells jingle
This is the weather when fingers tingle
This is the season when people mingle.

The new beginning comes with spring
The leaves turn green and the birds all sing
The early sun shows its shy, shiny face
The cobwebs glisten like golden lace
Now it's sunny with warmer rain
This is when people come out again.

Sunny summer comes at last
Bringing the warmth so very fast
The heat haze shimmers, the nights are light
Our skin is tanned and our eyes are bright
So if I sit now and watch the rain
I know that the sun will shine again!

Sally Wade (9)
St John's CE Primary School, Burscough

Teacher No. 1

You my teacher you are the best

You my teacher you are better than
All the rest.

You my teacher you never stop to
Have a rest.

You my teacher you're on a busy
Quest.

You my teacher you are the best
Of all
You my teacher you never shout
But you call

You my teacher you are a tall
Grown flower.

You my teacher boy have you got
Funky power.

You my teacher have you just got a
Funky power or are you just a tall
Grown flower?

Kayleigh Sutherland (10)
St John's CE Primary School, Burscough

My Mum Is . . .

My mum is . . .
Very very friendly
and wears a big smile from ear to ear
she has an Irish accent like a leprechaun.

My mum is . . .
Quite tall and slinky slim
She has dark brown curly hair
like a lion's mane
and very beautiful.

My mum is . . .
She laughs a lot
and has a fair face
she walks very fast

PS
I love her loads!

James Powell (10)
St John's CE Primary School, Burscough

My Secret Friend

My secret friend is kind to me,
She makes me giggle and smile.

My secret friend.

When I am upset she comes
to me and makes me
happy and I smile.

My secret friend.

She tells jokes and she
has blue eyes like
blue ink.

*My secret friend is
  Emily!*

Rosie Burrell (10)
St John's CE Primary School, Burscough

Remember

Remember the days when I was there
Remember the dog barking away
When I said 'Shut up'
Remember when I was out when you called
Remember the day when I left you alone
Remember when I was a clown
Remember when I hated you
Remember when I loved you
Remember when I punched you
Remember when I kicked you
Remember when it was my birthday
Remember when I liked you
Remember when we were pals
Remember . . . we are best friends!

Samantha Lee (9)
St Mark's CE Primary School, Scarisbrick

At The Fairground

Bumper cars, bumper cars,
Crashing all about.
Roller coaster, roller coasters,
Make you want to shout.
Hook a duck, hook a duck,
Can you win a prize?
Haunted house, haunted house,
What's the next surprise?
The big wheel, big wheel,
Goes round and round,
What fun, what fun!
At the fairground.

Megan Claeys-Sheridan (10)
St Mark's CE Primary School, Scarisbrick

Holly Tree

Like the glittering sunset.
Crunching, crackling, soft.
Fresh crisp smell of autumn.
Like sweets in a shiny bag.
Evergreen, spiky, dazzling,
Enchanted leaf of life.
Like the smooth skin of a baby.
Blood, apples, cherries.
Like a miniature tomato rolling down the road.

Holly Jackson (10)
St Mark's CE Primary School, Scarisbrick

There Once Was A . . .

There once was a sleeping cat on the hay,
Snoozing where the little mice play.
The horse is in his field that day,
Where the ponies like to neigh, neigh, neigh.

As the farmer's wife brings in the tray,
Of cups of tea in the month of May.
'Soon the birds will come our way,'
That is what the children say.

Tanya Steele (10)
St Mark's CE Primary School, Scarisbrick

Dolphins

Dolphins swim
And dolphins play
Dolphins dream the day away
Laughing, playing, jumping, sleeping,
Dolphins dream the day away.

Nicola Ball (10)
St Mark's CE Primary School, Scarisbrick

Captured

Isolated, away from home with my sister -
Hiding in a cupboard
While the Nazis bomb overhead
I looked out of a mist filled window
Bang! Down came the door.
A flood of grey uniforms charged in.
Boom! Father skidding along the smashed floor
They were closing in on our area.
We were cornered, nowhere to go.
Captured.

Dragged off in a dark brown van.
Engine rattling in front and behind.
People trying to escape.
Thirty-five years on we met again
Like we weren't apart.
I try to forget those days now
But it still feels like yesterday.

Jonathan Rhodes (10)
St Mary's CE Primary School, Greenfield

My Dog Zebbi

As black as liquorice laces,
As mad as a mad hatter,
As bouncy as a jumping frog,
As cute as the cutest dog,
As greedy as a pig,
As shiny as a brand new wig,
As thin as the thinnest log,
That's my dog.

Evie Maxwell (9)
St Mary's CE Primary School, Greenfield

Me! Me! Me! Me! Me! Mine! Money!

There once was a girl called Beth
Her father was a chef
She got four pounds every week
She got this dosh from her mum and dad
Because she gave them no cheek
And when she got it she was very glad.

But this is how the story goes
And I can tell you now Beth ends up with lots of foes.

Now you've probably guessed they were posh,
But soon they had no dosh.
So every time Beth got some money,
Her family pinched it and it was not funny.

Soon Beth had had enough
Stop! reading it's about to get rough.
So Beth put some fake money in a jar,
Her family wouldn't get very far.

Beth Cavanagh (10)
St Mary's CE Primary School, Greenfield

Rabbit

Run, run, rabbit,
Jump, jump, rabbit,
Well done rabbit.

Bound, bound across the grass,
Fur, fur a huge white mass.

Run, run, rabbit,
Jump, jump, rabbit,
Well done rabbit.

Eat, eat, gobble down food,
Stretch, stretch, I love you.

Natalie Mallalieu (10)
St Mary's CE Primary School, Greenfield

Seasons

Winter, summer, spring and fall,
Why do I love these seasons?
There are more than just some reasons;
Honey, milk and winter moon,
It is beautiful, and up so soon.
Why, it is just past noon,
Snowflakes gleaming in the light,
Getting on with their long flight.

Gold as money, very sunny, summer is so pretty,
Oh I smell the old sea salt and hear the sound of a rushing sea, coming in and out at me.

Flowers, rain, and puddles deep,
Easter eggs will get a heap!
Grass is ever so moist.

Yes this is a colourful season,
Happy and free of treason,
Jump, fall, squishy landing,
Friends are having time to play.

So these are the reasons that I love seasons.
Winter, summer, spring and fall.

Daniela Soldner (10)
St Mary's CE Primary School, Greenfield

School

S chool is boring
C ause everybody thinks so
H ere at school we have to do work
O h no here it comes
O h no it's literacy
'L isten, listen,' says the teacher
    Help

Phew it was only a dream.

Amelia Fenlon (9)
St Mary's CE Primary School, Greenfield

The Animal Limerick

There was a dog called Rusty,
Who liked the clown called Krusty,
He ate jelly,
While watching the telly,
And smelled extremely musty.

There was a cat called Bea,
Who was always waiting for tea,
She went outside,
And started to hide,
That daring young cat called Bea.

There was a rabbit called Grabbit,
Who had a terrible habit,
To beg at the door,
And ask for some more,
That was the rabbit called Grabbit.

Lewis Ralph (8)
St Mary's CE Primary School, Greenfield

My Bruvver And Me

M any inches bigger than me
Y et he makes me feel so tall.

B rave he is and very kind
R eady to catch me when I fall
U pside down and on the floor
V ertical ramps he just wants more
V ery good at skateboard tricks is he
E very day he plays with me
R eady to give his love for free.

A nytime I am lonely he is
N ever far away
D oing his best to cheer me up

M aking me laugh
E ach and every day.

Christopher Shawmarsh-Smith (8)
St Mary's CE Primary School, Greenfield

We Are Climbing

We are climbing a magic tree,
We are sailing a mighty sea,
We are running for Olympic gold,
We are getting a mighty scold, in the race for gold.

We are swimming in a big pool,
We are fed up of going to school.
I am going to have to go,
To my first ever show.

The teachers were insane
One of them had a pet lion
It had a beautiful mane
The machines were iron.

As you can see I have broken my arm,
At least the lion did no harm.

Andrew Marsden (10)
St Mary's CE Primary School, Greenfield

Mangoes With Banjos

(To the tune of 'Bananas in Pyjamas')

Mangoes with banjos are falling down the stairs,
Mangoes with banjos are kicking down fairs,
Mangoes with banjos are scaring teddy bears.

Boys with toys are very, very bright,
Boys with toys, never ever fight,
Boys with toys burn down their school.

Knights who have fights are very good at sports,
Knights who have fights had very good forts,
Knights who have fights are nearly now extinct.

Adam Smalley (10)
St Mary's CE Primary School, Greenfield

Where Are You?

I saw you a minute ago
I saw you a second ago
Where have you gone?

I will look round the corner
I will look down that street
Where have you gone?

Are you under a bush?
Are you behind a tree?
Where have you gone?

Are you here?
Are you there?
Are you anywhere?
Where have you gone?

Hey, what's that jiggling among the
leaves, let's go and see . . .
Ha! Found you.

Hannah Claydon (7)
St Mary's CE Primary School, Greenfield

Well You Shouldn't Have . . .

'Mum - I've just had an explosion,'
'Well, you shouldn't have shaken our drink!'

'Mum - I've just flooded the bathroom,'
'Well, you shouldn't have blocked up the sink!'

'Mum - I've just broken Grandad's fishing rod,'
'Well, you shouldn't have been in the shed!'

'Mum - I've just tidied my bedroom,'
'Well, you shouldn't have . . .
What's that you said?'

Thomas Woolley (9)
St Mary's CE Primary School, Greenfield

Goodbye

Today is the day, dusk is upon
Never will I see my sister again,
Nor my mum.
As we walk down the path
Where my sister and I once played
All our happy memories start to fade.
We walk to the station house,
With tears in our eyes
They say the war is upon us,
If we stay we will die.
You go to Scotland, I go to Wales,
In those days we're apart, I don't want you drinking ale.
I never saw my sister again
So I have one thing to say.
The 9th of December that was the day,
The journey began when the snow wasted away.

Faith Stanford (10)
St Mary's CE Primary School, Greenfield

Food

I love food,
My mum does too.
We are famous in our family
For my mum's special stew.

Burgers, chips and sausages too,
The ketchup pizza, got to add it's new.
Roast potatoes, meat pie,
Pancakes that fly up sky high.
Wibbly wobbly jelly on a plate,
Catch it quickly . . . whoops too late!

Joel Stanton (9)
St Mary's CE Primary School, Greenfield

Spelling Tests

Spelling tests are awful
especially for me,
they come every Friday morning,
and take longer than can be.

I hate those longer words,
like archaeology,
but shorter words I like,
like, 'buzz' or 'went' or 'be'.

When my teacher reads them out,
my fingers tense with fear,
too scared if I won't get them right,
too scared if I won't hear!

Spelling tests are awful,
especially for me,
so please stop saying those *big* words,
and leave me to play in peace!

Emma Stagg (10)
St Mary's CE Primary School, Greenfield

Robin Hood In Hollywood!

Robin Hood was in a wood
Not any wood but Hollywood.
Full of buildings, planes and cars not trees and
leaves and bits of bark.
What a strange place to be in.

Later on in the wood I came across Mr Hood.
But not in brown tights or a camouflaged coat.
But in a tuxedo and a posh speedboat.

Cameron Maxwell (10)
St Mary's CE Primary School, Greenfield

Wild Animals

Though the dodo is extinct
at this time,
I believe they're still out there,
Hey! This is a rhyme!

The bird of New Zealand
is the kiwi
only a bird,
walking next to me.

The aardvark has a silly name
it is very funny,
eats the termites all around,
but it doesn't eat honey.

King of the Jungle
lion of pride,
it's sometimes hungry
you'd better hide!

Black and white
is the colour
of the little tapir
who stays with his big brother.

It's super slippery,
very fast,
the moray eel
never finishes last.

James Moore (10)
St Mary's CE Primary School, Greenfield

Dear Family

I've been captured by the Nazis,
But I know how to get away,
I might get shot by the guards,
It's a chance I'll have to take.

Now I've got past the defenders,
I am nearly out of the base,
I killed one of the guards for his gun,
You know, just in case.

I don't know where I am going,
I am in the back of a truck,
The windows are all muddy,
But don't worry too much.

We have been sent out in groups,
Fifty people max,
I won't get killed, I promise,
So just sit back and relax.

Benjamin Rothery (9)
St Mary's CE Primary School, Greenfield

In The Park

Pretty roses flowing in the breeze,
Leaves floating down from the trees,
Sounds of the swings rattling together,
Sunlight shining,
Sound of children playing,
Birds cheeping in the trees,
The park is surrounded by beautiful things.

Katie Gartside (9)
St Mary's CE Primary School, Greenfield

Friends

F riends are the best
R eally reliable
I respect them for what they do for me
E nergetic and enjoyable
N oisy and loud
D o the best they can
S upported and special.

Sophie Kemp (10)
St Mary's CE Primary School, Greenfield

My Max

A barking leader
A bone chewer
A dashing runner
A kind thinker
A meat eater
A black and white jumper
That's my Max . . .

Rebecca Childs (11)
St Mary's CE Primary School, Greenfield

Snake

S neaks around
N early killed it, the silly mouse
A mazingly quick
K een learner
E nergetic snake.

Christian Shoel (9)
St Mary's CE Primary School, Greenfield

The Family Of Pigs

The rose of the jungle
covered in red
Red River Hog's his name,
And he lives in a shed.

The big fat bush pig
Covered in brown,
He digs for truffles
In the middle of town.

A pig from Sulawesi
Without any fur,
Babirusa's got an illness
And he's got the cure.

A Visayan warty pig
Is quite nice
He'll be your friend
But never give him rice.

So you've met all these pigs
And what they're like
They all like truffles
And roasted pike.

Jonathan Beilby (9)
St Mary's CE Primary School, Greenfield

The Runaway Pig

The runaway pig had hatched a plan
To save himself from becoming ham!
His plan was to escape from the farm
And save himself from any harm.

He made his escape at the top of Mount Doom!
He jumped off and landed safely at noon.
I've told you his story, so please don't tell,
That the runaway pig was successful!

David Lyons (11)
St Mary's CE Primary School, Greenfield

Animal Alphabet

A ngry alligators
B eautiful bears
C heeky chimps
D ozy donkeys
E legant elephants
F unny frogs
G ood gorillas
H ungry horse
I ll iguanas
J umping jellyfish
K icking kangaroos
L eaping leopards
M ischievous monkeys
N aughty newts
O bedient octopus
P erfect peacock
Q uarking quails
R ude rabbits
S inging snake
T ired turtle
U gly unicorns
V icious vermin
W hinging whales
X 'cellent X-ray fish
Y apping yak
Z esty zebra.

Sophie Paterson (9)
St Mary's CE Primary School, Greenfield

Lizard

He creeps on a rock
Scouting for a desert rat
It scampers away
Relentlessly he tries on
And spies another innocent rat.

Robert Edwards (11)
St Mary's CE Primary School, Greenfield

Living Or Dead?

Going out one Saturday night
Just like a normal schoolgirl,
But the question lies . . . will she return?

The next few days passed
Slow as growing grass,
But where is our lovely Lucy?

Days turned to weeks,
And weeks turned to months,
But nowhere to be seen was our Lucy.

Tears were shed,
And thoughts were flying,
But was she living or was she dead?

Investigations were carried out,
And still little Lucy was not found,
But then they found the body . . .

Drowned in the bath,
At her best friend's house,
But to the family's horror, it was her dad that did it.

So through the golden gates of Heaven
Went our little Lucy,
Without saying a final goodbye.

Jessica Shaw (10)
St Mary's CE Primary School, Greenfield

Mrs Conner

A good singer,
A groovy mover,
A caring mother,
A joke cracker,
A husband lover,
A cuddly teacher,
A careful listener.

Natalie Burgess (10)
St Mary's CE Primary School, Greenfield

Pets Galore

Twelve pets running round the house,
Every pet except a mouse.
Trying not to mess up the living room
But it'll be a bomb site soon.

A bird in a corner, sitting in its cage,
A circus bird, it made the front page.
A puppy, called Sam, wagging its tail,
Went to the door to chew up the mail.

A cat, sitting purring, on the settee,
Oh no! The kitten's gone to have a wee!
A hamster running on its wheel,
Oops, I forgot to give it its daily meal!

A corn snake through the grass so timid,
I found it in Egypt, near a pyramid.
A gorilla in the closet, always in its prime,
Phew! I'm glad it's nearly bedtime!

Rebecca Bell (11)
St Mary's CE Primary School, Greenfield

What Animals Do

The wombat is great at digging,
The chinchilla can hop and hop,
The gibbon is great in the trees,
The cheetah runs at very fast speeds,
That is what these animals do.

The numbat likes to eat ants
The wolverine eats moose and elk
The tiger is king, of the cats,
The golden eagle swoops very fast
That is what these animals do.

Andrew Walford (9)
St Mary's CE Primary School, Greenfield

A Baby

A cute cuddler
A dung dropper
A raspberry blower
A bottle drinker
A diaper stinker
A milk waster
A thumb sucker
A silent sleeper.

Lawrence Copson (11)
St Mary's CE Primary School, Greenfield

Kitten

A snow purrer
A caring friend
A food scrambler
A swift pounder
A delightful player
A graceful sleeper
A soft cuddler
A scary kisser.

Gemma Barlow (10)
St Mary's CE Primary School, Greenfield

Rainbow

A giant oval
A blast of colours
A floating picture
A colour fountain
A weather mix
A gold source
A wave of jewels
A treasure chest.

Bethany Kippax (11)
St Mary's CE Primary School, Greenfield

Love At First Sight

Innocently I ran down the platform to the man I love!
He held me tight and didn't let go.
I asked 'How did you find me?'
He replied 'I always knew where you were.'
The man I love gave me a ring and said 'So?'
I was shocked and the words were, 'Yes of course!'
He told me about how long it took to get the ring.
We sat down on a bench nearby.
After a while I noticed my train had gone
But my lover told me to go home with him!
I gave him the key to my heart.

Hayley Lockeridge (11)
St Mary's CE Primary School, Greenfield

Times Of The Year

Springtime, springtime, daffodils are rising and the sun is shining,
Children are playing out, and birds are singing.

Summertime, summertime, the sun is fully out,
Children at the beach are digging out sand.

Autumn, autumn, leaves are falling,
Children are going in and Hallowe'en is haunting.

Winter, winter, snow is falling, children are making snowmen
And having several cups of hot chocolate a day.

Megan Fahy (7)
St Mary's CE Primary School, Greenfield

Horse

H air flying in the wind
O pen nostrils flaring
R unning wild and free
S addle, reins, girth and all
E yes flashing happily.

May Wall (8)
St Mary's CE Primary School, Greenfield

Black Tear

One night I lay in bed
Dark, cold, lonely.
I was scared, alone, I sighed.
On my own, in the dark, at night.
I didn't move.
I stayed motionless, taut, tense.
No wonder I was alone, abandoned.
I'd been evil; used the wrong powers to rule
But my plans failed,
The objectors caught me.
I was sent to a small cell
On its own; a capsule in Ireland.
No furniture apart from a bed:
Stone cold and rock hard
So they sent me here
And,
As I remember,
I cry
A
Black tear.

Elizabeth Shoel (11)
St Mary's CE Primary School, Greenfield

There Was A Young Lady . . .

There was a young lady called Nancy,
Who thought herself quite fancy.
She had rings on her toes
And a bell on her nose!
That eccentric young lady called Nancy.

Amy Winterbottom (10)
St Mary's CE Primary School, Greenfield

Seashore Shell

Washed up with driftwood
Onto a desolate, forgotten coast
Golden green or white
A horn or tusk, twisted shape.

Among beautiful shells
With sensational colours and shapes
Gold among silver
A planet collected with stars.

A shining, shimmering coastline,
This shell, the centrepiece
A diamond encrusted with pearls
A coast admired by all who see it.

Benjamin Hall (11)
St Mary's CE Primary School, Greenfield

What Animals Can Do

Cats can miaow
Dogs can run
Frogs can leap and
Have good fun
Tigers can prowl
Lions can eat
Mice are the little things bats can beat
Monkeys are like humans in every single way
The way they love their babies when they hug them and play.
Hedgehogs sleep in a ghostly wood and huddle under a
spiky bush.

Eleanor Butterworth (8)
St Mary's CE Primary School, Greenfield

Local Language

'It's a grand day,' mi father said,
'So wake up, sleepyhead
Get yourself out of that old fleapit
I'll take thee for a walk in a little bit.

Get on your cardi and yer hat
And thi clogs - ow about that?
Up them 'ills and up t' top
Walk, walk, never stop.

We'll take a butty and some pie
A bit of tripe but I don't know why.
At the top we'll admire the view
We'll enjoy it - just me and you.'

Toby Jones (8)
St Mary's CE Primary School, Greenfield

Goodbye, Goodbye

It was misty and wintry,
With snow on the road,
Today is the day we depart on our own,
To Scotland, to Wales, that's where we'll go
Forever and ever we'll be alone.

At last the war is over,
And peace is here again.
I'm waiting at the station to get back
on the train
And now the time has come,
I'm going home to meet my sister,
My dad and my mum.

Nina Jones (10)
St Mary's CE Primary School, Greenfield

Nonsense

N onsense things are very strange
O ctopus wearing oval slippers
N yalas wearing five feet flippers
S ometimes they look silly from a range
E veryday they are quite funny
N ever do they stay the same
S illy is their favourite game
E veryone of them has not got a name!

James Wright (8)
St Mary's CE Primary School, Greenfield

Brownies

We go to Brownies when we are seven
Everyone says it's Heaven.

We get enrolled
when we are told.

We have lots of fun
and get a lot done.

From making
to baking
and reading
to weeding.

Brown Owl is the boss
but she never gets cross.

We have smiley faces
when we go to places.

We do badges and sing,
have fun in everything.

Zoe Molyneux (9)
St Peter's CE Junior School, Leigh

Strawberry Moose

There was a strawberry moose
that was on the loose,
he was very cheeky
and he ran rather weirdly.
He had strawberries all over his head,
which he squashed when he was in bed.
He made a terrible mess
that gave people alot of stress.
So if you want an easier life
never make a moose your wife!

Christopher Hamer (9)
St Peter's CE Junior School, Leigh

Into My Opinion

One day I went into my opinion
And I met a boy named Minion.
He had brown hair with a strange scientific coat
and little round glasses.
My opinion is sort of weird in different ways.
He took me to tea and served with trays,
He was very annoying,
It was so good to be out of my opinion,
And away from Minion.

Chloe McDonough (9)
St Peter's CE Junior School, Leigh

The Simpsons

When the Simpsons came out I loved it.
It was funnier than I had imagined.
I watch and watch and nothing can stop me.
I bought it on video and it was fantastic.

Becky Abbott (9)
St Peter's CE Junior School, Leigh

If I Was A Fairy

If I was a fairy I would fly high in the sky
I would flutter all around making sure my family and friends
were all right.
If I was a fairy I would cast lots of nice spells
Waving my magic wand being good to everyone.
If I was a fairy I would flutter over hills flying to and fro
Doing lots of nice things.
If I was a fairy I would be good to everyone
So they would say what a good fairy, I am.

Laura Balmer (9)
St Peter's CE Junior School, Leigh

Winter Warmth

One warm hat,
two cold cheeks,
ten cheeky fingers,
ten toasty toes,
ten chilly fingers,
ten toasty toes,
two warm ears,
and one cold nose!

Lauren Ashbrook (8)
St Peter's CE Junior School, Leigh

Snow Everywhere

Snow everywhere
On the church,
On the trees
On the roofs.

I see white on the walls
In holes
On the floor
I see snow everywhere

Justin Burns (9)
St Peter's CE Junior School, Leigh

If I Was An Alien!

If I was an alien,
I could fly,
Up high in the sky,
Eating a pizza pie.

I could be a rabbit,
With a bad habit.

I could act like a dog
sitting on a log.
Next to a frog and a hog!

If I was an alien
I could be a cat on a mat
I could be a rat or a bat too
. . . But I'm not one!

Sarah Dean (9)
St Peter's CE Junior School, Leigh

The Snow Day

Down in the field
Where the rabbits play
Snow came down yesterday
Me and myy friend went down to see
Everything was covered in snow
I put on my hat and my gloves
Then I had a snowball fight
Everything was cold
I went over to the pond
And skated there all day long.

Bryoni Parkinson (9)
St Peter's CE Junior School, Leigh

If I Were A . . .

If I were a dog I would lick people
If I were a parrot I would copy my mum.
If I were a soldier I would shoot people.
If I were a cat I would scratch people.
If I were a monkey I would eat bananas.
If I were a rabbit I would eat carrots.

If I were a giraffe
I would give my brother
A ride on my head!

Kimberly Blackburn (9)
St Peter's CE Junior School, Leigh

Our Classroom

Dear Jean
I'm a classroom
I get things put on my walls
Sharp, sharp, sharp 'ouch'
It hurts very much.

Computers and televisions
Tables and chairs
Pencils and pens
Books and dictionaries.

Comics and tissues
Pegs and coats
Bags and sportswear
Music and posters
These are the things that get put into me.

I don't like being a classroom
It's a horrible job
Teachers start shouting
Children start crying
That's what happens to me.

Deborah Norris (9)
Withnell Fold Primary School

New Classroom!

I have just about
Had enough,
I really, really can't wait.

We never have anything to do
At playtime,
(That's me and my friend Kate).

Half our football pitch
Is covered up,
With sand and stone and bricks.

All put to one side,
Which the builders are
Going to mix.

The builders said
It would be ready
It wouldn't take long to build.

It is now four months late,
And still
We can't play!

Nikki Evans (11)
Withnell Fold Primary School

Snow

As I wandered through children playing
Red noses and tingling hands
Older children throwing ice-cold snow
Younger children building snowmen
Everything is glistening white
Oh I hope this day will last forever.

Chelsea Waterhouse (9)
Withnell Fold Primary School

The Builders Are Extremely Slow

The builders are extremely slow
I want to know when they will go
The corridors are very dusty
The classrooms are cold and musty
The hammers banging
The fencing clanging.

The builders are extremely slow
I want to know when they will go
Our Internet cable has completely gone
Their radio is always on
The hammers banging
The fencing clanging.

The builders are extremely slow
I want to know when they will go
I don't like the builders at all
Because when they're here we can't play football
The hammers banging
The fencing clanging.

Danielle Jackson (10)
Withnell Fold Primary School

Builders

Wood and
Everything that's
Known to man is in this
Playground because of the builders
Building.

Crash bang
Falling rocks, bricks
Slates and lots, lots more
Because of the hopeless builders
Building.

Luke Davy (11)
Withnell Fold Primary School

Seasons

Spring
Animals mating
Butterflies fly
Lovely colours
Young lambs will come
Flash! They came.

Summer
Young lambs staggering
Stumbling about
We catch minnows
And we catch trout
Dinner served.

Autumn
All the frost-crisped leaves
Fall from the trees
With a dry crack
Tumble from trees
Onto the ground.

Winter
Rivers standing still
Stationary
Bare trees, bare woods
Deprived of leaves
All life dead.

Charlie Patterson (10)
Withnell Fold Primary School

Builders Working

Builders working with slates and stones
They're working on top of the roof
If they fall down they'll break their bones
They're wearing warm jeans and rough coats.

The builders are strong but being very slow
We can't concentrate on our work
I hope that they won't take very much longer
They said they'd be finished quite soon.

The builders are making the new classroom
So we can't play football anymore
They work from morning until noon
They work with drills and ladders.

The builders are working on the scaffolding
With the poles and hammers
The builders are nearly always singing
I hope they do finish quite soon.

James Hopkin (10)
Withnell Fold Primary School

Slow Builders

Builders working very slow
Wires poking in and out
Climbing ladders
Hammering nails
Slate carrying but not all day
Cement mixers, glass fixers
Slow builders
Drinking cups of tea
Not much work being done
Slow builders
Fencing for children
To keep them out
Don't be so slow
Slow builders.

Elizabeth Jones (10)
Withnell Fold Primary School

Building Work

The builders haven't finished yet,
But months ago they said,
'It'll be finished in October 03'
More like two thousand and ten.

I come to school in the morning,
It's the same sight at night,
Ugly scaffolding, ugly builders,
It would give anyone a fright.

They're working on the new classroom,
supposedly so,
they've broken off our Internet,
why can't they just go?

They're getting very tedious now,
We're all very fed up,
their clothes are never very smart,
as they're always covered in muck.

Edward Melling (10)
Withnell Fold Primary School

Builders Working On Our Roof

Builders working on our roof
In their jeans and waterproofs
Scruffy clothes and great big blocks
Sometimes they even wear odd socks.
When will they go? I just don't know
But it had better be soon.
Perhaps they'll go before the next blue moon
Do they really have to stay?
Oh how I wish they'd go away
I do not like the builders at all
Because I want them to go
Surely you must feel my woe.

Allan Struthers (10)
Withnell Fold Primary School

The Bears

Today I saw a baby bear
Snuggling against its mother
His face was cute and chubby
Just like his charming brother.

Their mother clutched them closer
With her powerful but gentle paws
The cubs snuggled into her fluffy tummy
Showing their small white claws.

I could see she loved her cubs dearly
And would keep them safe forever
She pulled them closer with one little tap,
As if they were a feather.

But as I stood there staring
The mother began to awake
Only then I realised
She could turn like a vicious snake.

Maria Peck (11)
Withnell Fold Primary School

Building Works

Bricks fed up of being
Stuck together
Ladders fed up of being
Climbed up
With bootmarks in a line.
Drills drilling holes in the wall
Making a terrible noise
Paste being splattered
On the wallpaper
Nails being knocked in bricks
Cement chucked in buckets
Forklifts lifting heavy objects.

Alexander Snape (9)
Withnell Fold Primary School

The House Of Gloom

Creeping through this house so small,
Even an echo sounds like a call.
For he was here around this house,
But all I can see is a little mouse.
Floorboards creak and,
The pitter-patter of the kitchen leak.
He was here I sense him now,
I don't know where I don't know how.
All I know is this house so bare,
Is similar to a lion's lair.
All around I sense the fear,
Too scared and petrified to cry a tear.
In this haunted and ghastly place,
My footsteps you would be too scared to trace.
I creep down the dusty hallways,
I hope these won't be the last of my days.
I hear a voice behind the door,
I am frightened right to the core.
I retrace my steps back to the door,
And cut across the country moor.
I hope that no one goes back there,
To that house so dark and bare.

Shona Jackson (9)
Withnell Fold Primary School